On Being Jewish Now

On Being Jewish Now

Edited by Zibby Owens

with the Founding Team of
Artists Against Antisemitism

ZIBBY BOOKS
NEW YORK

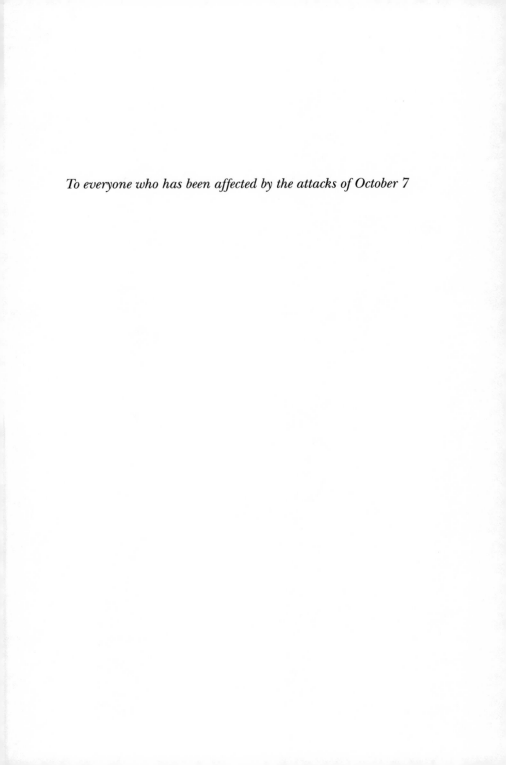

To everyone who has been affected by the attacks of October 7

CONTENTS

Introduction

Zibby Owens

Why We're All Here

I never planned to be "publicly Jewish," as many now refer to those of us who have used our platforms to advocate for fellow Jews. I mean, I'd never *hidden* that I was Jewish. It just wasn't the most salient part of my personality, nor was it overly relevant to the mainstream conversations I was having on social media, on my podcast, or in my newsletters about books. Of course, I included books by Jewish authors when I loved them and wanted to shout about them from the rooftops, but not disproportionately to books by other authors. A book was a book was a book.

Sometimes I'd post about Judaism when the spirit moved me: a photo of candles I'd remembered to light that Shabbat. A beautiful Passover table. The Hanukkah festivities. I did write an essay about the Pittsburgh massacre, which fell on a night when I was at a friend's daughter's bat mitzvah. I also wrote about my deepening connection to my own temple during the pandemic after the loss of my mother-in-law and grandmother-in-law to COVID, and the loss of my own BFF grandmother. Suddenly, *our* family was the one receiving gifts and calls. Our loved ones' names were being read and honored on *yahrzeit*, the anniversary of their deaths.

I made the main character in my debut novel Jewish, because of course I did. *Write what you know.* It wasn't even a conscious decision to make Pippa Jewish; she just *was.* I included a lockdown scene at a temple and gave the Hebrew school teacher a big role because Pippa's son was preparing for his bar mitzvah. I even named the teacher's dog Dayenu because: funny!

Although I hadn't been a regular "poster" about Judaism specifically, I realized that as my nonexistent social media accounts became fulsome and my public identity went from complete nobody to someone who could potentially help others, I didn't feel fear in speaking out about things I believed in.

I speak out because I feel things incredibly deeply. Pain. Hurt. Unfairness. Joy. All of it. If a good piece of cake makes someone else happy, it makes me so ecstatic that I moan in delight and ask to talk to the baker and tell everyone about it. Likewise, when someone wrongs me or someone I love, I pounce.

Another reason I speak out, I think (although I'm not totally sure; call my old therapist), is that I feel the shortness of life, constantly. I was born with a heightened awareness of my own mortality, but losing my best friend and college roommate on 9/11 hammered it home for me. At any moment, I could disappear in a puff of smoke like she did. As the children's line goes, "Hare today, goon tomorrow." When I go to lunch at a new restaurant, I share my location in case the restaurant blows up in a targeted explosion and

I disappear. When I cross the street, I'm wondering who will know to call my kids if I get hit by a car. Anxiety or reality? Who cares? Given this fire in my soon-to-expire belly, I act. If I have a business idea, I start it. If I have a book idea, I write it. If I see a problem in an industry, I try to solve it. Pandemic hits? Start an Instagram Live show. Boom.

So when October 7 happened, I cried, I mourned, and then I moved. I posted. I wrote about it. I acted. Before October 7, I hadn't experienced much antisemitism. Just a sprinkle of sea salt on a big buffet. Suddenly, I became one of the many targets. I lost followers and had people attack me about my decision to withdraw from the National Book Awards when I raised valid concerns about antisemitism. My name was added to blacklists of Jewish authors. An antisemitic troll tried to tank the Goodreads ranking for my novel before it even came out, but I garnered enough support from readers to get the spiteful comment "Zionist racist" taken down. Many guests who were scheduled to be on my podcast canceled. So many people—so many friends—just didn't understand the facts. If they did, I reasoned, there's *no way* they could be saying and thinking these things. *If they only understood!*

I was scared to speak out. I'm *still* scared. I was scared that asserting my Jewishness publicly would get me in trouble. (And it did.) But I knew I had to speak up. What would happen if I didn't? What if no one spoke up? I had a platform that I had to use. If I could, I must.

At every stop on my recent book tour, at least one woman would approach me. Timid. Quiet. She would wait until the signing line had ended and come over to me, nervously, and then whisper, "I just wanted to thank you for speaking out . . . for all you're doing . . . for the Jewish people."

I'd hear about her cousins or friends or colleagues who had been in Israel on October 7 or who had been lost. I'd hear about the antisemitic attacks in her neighborhood. How she hadn't been sleeping. How all she could do was worry about her kids. Shell-shocked, the woman would reiterate how much it meant to have another voice out there: my voice. How it kept her from feeling less alone.

"Thank you," she would say again. "Keep speaking out. We need you."

As I slipped my Sharpies back into my tote bag, collected my belongings, and thanked the bookstore owner or event host, all I could do was think about her.

I still am.

And so, this project.

I helped start up Artists Against Antisemitism, founded by Alison Hammer in the aftermath of October 7, with a group of fellow authors, some I knew, some new to me. Our group on Instagram has gotten me through many dark days.

One morning in late June, I wrote to the group: "Guys, I have an idea. What if we do an anthology of essays about our experiences and donate all the funds to Artists Against Antisemitism?" They enthusiastically said "Yes!" and volunteered to help. We invited more than two hundred authors and advocates to contribute essays, pro bono, to the collection within a few short weeks. Seventy-four said yes. (Many others would have written had it not been for the tight deadline, but I was determined to get the eBook out fast, at least by October 1, to commemorate the anniversary of the attacks.)

Editing this collection has been one of the most meaningful endeavors of my entire career. It wasn't just a procrastination effort from my second novel, which shared an end-of-July deadline, one that sadly I am missing for possibly the first time in my life. It was a lifeline.

Every time an essay would come in, I'd stop what I was doing to read it. Edit it. Send it off in a batch to copyedit. With every press of the keyboard as I worked on the documents, I was healing my soul. The staccato typing sounds were evidence that yes, there *was* something I could do: I could do *this*.

And I did.

Thank you so much to all the contributors for sharing their personal stories. Thanks to the Artists Against Antisemitism founding members team for their encouragement and contributions. Thanks to my Zibby Books team for getting this thing made in time, especially Anne Messitte, president of Zibby Media and publisher of Zibby Books, who made it all happen and whose counsel and guidance have been the most important thing ever. Also, thanks to Chelsea Grogan, our managing editor; Graça Tito, our cover designer; plus Paul Bogaards, Erinn McGrath, Samantha Marks, Jordan Blumetti, Alex Feigin, and *everyone* on the Zibby Media team. (You have *all* helped.) Thanks to Lisa Cahn of Prose Garden Audio for the audio editing, Morning Moon Music for the music, Two Rivers/Ingram for the quick distribution help, and Sophia Chabbott for the expert counsel. Personally, thanks to my four kids and Kyle for understanding why I spent most of my summer inside working on this project (sorry!) and to my entire family for being so supportive. And thanks to everyone who has made this book a book.

Mostly, thank you to YOU, the reader. Thank you for listening to our stories. Thank you for holding space for grief, humor, loss, reflection, and trauma. Thank you for putting yourself in our shoes. Thank you for taking your precious time to process our thoughts and feelings. Every sentence you read feels like a gift. I hope that reading it helps you, too, whatever your background, and reminds you that you aren't alone. I hope you share *your* thoughts.

My mom recently told me a story from when I was a little girl. We were at a restaurant, Sweet Basil, where she and a close friend were talking nonstop. When the conversation moved to something related to Judaism, their voices suddenly dropped.

I piped up and asked, "How come whenever you talk about Jewish things, you always lower your voice?"

The two of them exchanged a look.

My mother replied, "You're absolutely right. There's no reason for us to lower our voices. Thanks for pointing that out." She told this story when accepting a Jewish advocacy prize of her own decades ago.

I am not lowering my voice. Join me.

PART ONE

Jewish Pride
and Joy

Dara Kurtz

I'm Proud to Be Jewish, Now More Than Ever

"Who would hide us?" my twentysomething daughter asked my husband and me when she was home visiting. For weeks we had watched antisemitism grow at an alarming rate across the country, spreading like poison ivy.

"What?" I asked, shocked.

While my daughter hadn't had an antisemitic experience herself, she was feeling the strain of being Jewish, like we all were. My husband and I glanced at each other, caught off guard.

"You heard me," she continued. "If history repeats itself and if what happened to Grandma Margaret and Papa happens again, who do you think we could actually count on to hide us and keep us safe?"

She was referring to my father's family and how they were forced to flee Germany and the Nazis. Fortunately, my grandparents escaped and ended up in the United States. Many family members, however, including both sets of their parents, were murdered in concentration camps.

"I don't know," I told her. "I've honestly never thought about it before."

My husband nodded in agreement. What proceeded was an absurd conversation about possible non-Jewish friends who might be willing to risk their lives to hide us, their Jewish friends, should we need it.

"Do you think we could count on the X family?"

"No, I don't think so. How about the Y family?"

"Maybe. They reached out to me and have been supportive since October 7."

"The Z family posted positive things on social media, saying they stand with their Jewish friends. Perhaps they would?"

At the conclusion of this conversation, we had our list. It was small but mighty.

I tossed and turned in bed that night. Then I woke up my husband.

"Do you think we could *really* ever be in a situation where we have to hide?" I asked him.

"Hopefully not," he answered, half asleep. "But the Jews in Germany never thought they would be hiding, either."

Weeks later, we visited some out-of-town family members and went through my late grandfather's coin collection. It was fun to see it again; it had been stashed in my father's house for decades before it was appropriately transferred to a lockbox.

"What's this?" I asked, as I dug through one of the bags.

I held a large pill bottle in my hand. While my grandfather was a doctor, it was strange to find this bottle inside his coin collection. I opened it. There on top was a folded, tiny piece of paper. We all stopped what we were doing. I unfolded the letter and gasped at what I saw.

"It's a note from Grandpa!"

Written in my grandfather's perfectly neat handwriting was the following:

These gold coins are ¼ of those which were spirited out of Nazi Germany by family members and finally reached me after WW2. I gave the other ¾ to my three sisters. They are insurance against the breakdown of paper money.

Papa

"Wow. What a treasure," my brother said.

We thought about the journey these coins had made and the emotions behind the letter. Our grandfather had passed away decades ago. It was an incredible gift. We also couldn't believe the timing. With everything going on in the world, was this a reminder to be more proactive and to make sure we have things in place *should* history repeat itself?

It was a sobering thought.

I don't know what the future holds for Israel, for Jewish Americans, or for my family. What I do know is that since the horrific events of October 7, I have never been prouder to be Jewish. My grandfather's letter reminded me that my family's story, as hard and devastating as it was because of the Holocaust, was laced with strength and perseverance. My grandfather and his wife came to another country, worked hard, and made a beautiful life for themselves and future generations. I have the life I have today because of their determination. They didn't give up, and neither will I.

I bear the responsibility to raise my voice, to stand up for my convictions, and to choose hope instead of fear, not only for my family and myself, but also for the future of the

Jewish people. I know there are no guarantees for any of us. But between the kind text messages I have received from my non-Jewish friends (who just wanted me to know they're "thinking of me and hurting with me") to the deep and meaningful conversations I've had with my Jewish friends, I don't feel like I'm walking this path alone. Instead, I feel loved and supported, connected to friends and family, and grateful to be Jewish. While it isn't always easy, I wouldn't change who I am for anything.

DARA KURTZ is the author of *I Am My Mother's Daughter: Wisdom on Life, Loss, and Love*; *Crush Cancer*; and *Living with Gratitude*. Dara's been a guest on more than seventy podcasts/TV/radio shows and speaks often to large corporations, colleges, and nonprofits. Her personal blog, *Crazy Perfect Life*, reaches more than two hundred thousand followers. She has been published on *Newsweek*'s "My Turn," *Moms Don't Have Time to Grieve*, *Scary Mommy*, Kveller, *Authority Magazine*, HuffPost, *Grown & Flown*, *Today Parenting*, and many others. Her goal is to use her life experiences to help people strengthen their relationships and create more happiness and joy in their everyday lives.

Jeremy Garelick

On Being Jewish

I walked into AJ's gun shop. I turned to my wife, Sam, with a weird smile on my face. She looked back at me, like, "What the hell are we doing here?"

We're New York Jews in a gun shop. What do we know about guns? We know about bagels, about Roth IRAs, about Hamantaschen . . . but guns?

"What kinda gun are you looking for?" asked Adam, the owner. No clue. "You want something for bears? For deer? Target practice?" We didn't know how to answer.

"We're Jewish," Sam said.

Adam stared at us for a moment, sizing us up, an uneasy tension in the air. Then, spoken with clear confidence, he said, "You're gonna want a nine-millimeter Beretta and pump-action shotgun."

I never thought I'd be a gun owner, but I also never thought I'd be woken up by my wife on the morning of October 7, with her saying: "Israel was attacked. It's bad."

Last June, my family moved from Los Angeles, where I could trip and fall into a minyan, to a small town in

Upstate New York, where I am the call for the tenth man when a minyan is needed. There are no kosher restaurants and the Jewish community is made up mostly of my wife's family. The responsibility of being Jewish is more challenging here because we have to represent all the Jewish people to everyone.

My oldest son is one of the only Jewish students in his public school. (In fact, he's attending Christian Brothers next year, where there are actually more Jews.) I was nervous about how he'd respond going into class on Monday, October 9. After all, he was a freshman in a new public high school on the other side of the country. I had channeled my own mom with a pep talk that I was ready to give about how he should be a strong, proud Jew and a strong, proud Zionist (by the way, his name is Zion). He came down from his room in a Krav Maga T-shirt with Hebrew letters. The tears ran down my face. I didn't have to give him a speech. It was already in him.

For better or worse, it was already in all of us: our Jewish pride, our love of Israel, our generational trauma, our anxiety, our need to make sure that our grandmothers would be proud of how we acted at all times, and our lack of ability to be okay when other Jews are not okay. Like so many Jews since October 7, I am not okay. I smile. I laugh. I work. I write. But I'm faking it. Underneath all of it, I am anxious, scared, heartbroken for the hostages and their families. I feel horribly guilty that I am in a position of influence, yet can't do anything to bring them home.

On top of that horrible feeling of inadequacy and guilt, I feel an insane burden to defend the actions of Israel to everyone around me, which makes me feel like I'm going crazy.

How can so many people justify the actions of Hamas? What is everyone seeing that I can't see? What the hell is wrong with me? Was everything I was taught wrong? Was everything I saw with my own eyes wrong?

Since October 7, I have witnessed inexplicable antisemitism. The kind I've always studied that I never understood. The kind that made Pharoah, Haman, Hitler, and so many others attempt to destroy us. The kind that was, well, inexplicable.

I open up Instagram and see images of Jews stabbed, shuls burned, kosher restaurants vandalized, schools being shot at—and I see the people I work with and call "friends" remaining silent. I look at silence as a positive. Why? So many others in my sphere are actively promoting antisemitism. Staying silent about it has become a welcomed trait. I've actively thanked my Middle Eastern coworkers for *not* sharing death-to-Jews-like posts.

My Hebrew name is Shalom, which means peace. I've been all about conflict resolution for my entire life, but being Jewish now means that I have to be vigilant and strong. I have to be prepared for the fact that people I've loved, helped, and trusted might inexplicably dislike my family and me just because we're Jewish.

I now understand how society let my Bubby's parents get murdered in front of her eyes, her father's beard ripped from his face. Like it or not, I'm Jewish. And somehow, Sam's simple response to Adam's question about what kind of gun we were looking for made so much more sense.

Like my Bubby and Queen Esther and Moses and Joshua and countless others before me, people will inexplicably hate me for being Jewish. And like Pharoah, Hitler, and

Haman, those who try to destroy us won't succeed, and our great-great-grandchildren will have a holiday about it, where they will eat and dance and close the night by singing, "Next year in Jerusalem!" Let it be so.

JEREMY GARELICK is a prolific writer-director known for *Murder Mystery 2, The Break-Up, The Wedding Ringer,* and *The Hangover,* and for founding American High, a company that has utilized innovative production and tech to reinvent the teen comedy and has produced sixteen films over the past five years.

Jeremy has also helmed numerous original TV series, including Netflix's *Best. Worst. Weekend. Ever.* His company's American High Digital amassed more than a million followers in under a year. The Academy at American High, his nonprofit founded in 2018, has supported more than nine hundred interns and has provided accessible film education to many.

Bradley Tusk

Why Being Jewish Matters

My girlfriend, Laurel, and I went to Montreal for the weekend. After we got to the airport, thunderstorms struck New York, and our flight home was canceled. We decided to rent a car and drive back, but everything was taken. As we were standing in the very crowded rental car facility absorbing the reality of having to do this all over again the next day, we overheard a woman around our age asking someone else if they were going to New York. It turns out they had rented a twelve-person passenger van and were looking for people to split the driving and the cost.

Get in a van with strangers? Aren't our entire childhoods designed to prevent that very thing? Cross an international border with people you've never met? Do I look like I have a hole in my head?

I glanced at the couple at the counter dealing with the van rental. The man had tattoos running up and down his arms and legs. Lots of them. Including a Star of David on his right calf. I walked closer. They both had IDF dog tags hanging around their necks. They spotted the Star of David around my neck, pointed, smiled, and nodded.

"I never wore this until October 7," I volunteered. "But after that, I figured, I'm proud of who I am. I'm not hiding anything." They were exactly the same—neither of them was Israeli, but both were Jewish. Laurel and I got in the van. And made it back just fine. (In fact, all things considered, it was lovely.)

I grew up mainly on Long Island. I went to Penn. I've lived most of my adult life in Manhattan. I really have not experienced antisemitism. But I'm also the grandson of Holocaust survivors. My grandparents and father came to this country after spending years living in the Displaced Persons camps in postwar Germany, waiting for someone to sponsor them to come to the U.S. (or Israel or South America—they would have gone anywhere that would have taken them). My family was always grateful to live in this country but never 100 percent sure that Jews would be safe here long-term. Nothing against the U.S., but we had never lasted indefinitely in *any* country or culture, no matter how good things seemed at the time. So I grew up seeing Israel as more than a cultural or religious homeland. I saw it as an insurance policy—this is where you go if things turn bad here.

Post–October 7, I honestly can't decide if things are genuinely bad here or not. Sometimes I read the news and feel like Jews are being hunted one by one. Sometimes it feels like we're entering the beginning of the end. But more often than not, it feels okay.

I teach at Columbia, and while the tents and protests were both awful and undeniable, I didn't see any of that sentiment

BRADLEY TUSK

from my students. Like many Jews in New York, I donated to George Latimer in his primary campaign against Jamaal Bowman and saw unity across the Jewish community leading to his resounding defeat.

I own a bookstore on the Lower East Side called P&T Knitwear, and even while many of our customers' politics are left wing, our Jewish culture (the original P&T was the store my grandfather and a friend of his from the DP camps started in 1952 on Allen Street) is highlighted and celebrated daily. My kids go to a Quaker school that's pretty progressive, but neither has experienced anything resembling antisemitic or anti-Israeli indoctrination. (My son and I have read the *New York Post* together every morning for years, so he is a proud defender of Israel.)

I don't want to be naïve. Antisemitism is very real and there's no guarantee Jews will be safe here forever. But amid the fear, amid the anxiety, the protests and accusations and anger, also comes purpose.

Because being Jewish matters. And doing the things that make being Jewish worthwhile—tzedakah, teshuvah, tefillah—matter more than ever. Jews have always focused on helping others. Jews have always focused on community, on civic engagement, on standing up for what's right. Jews have always focused on ideas, on intellect, on creating and making things, from paintings, to vaccines, to skyscrapers.

Considering we're just 0.2 percent of the global population, Jews have contributed more to society than any other ethnicity by an exponentially disproportionate amount.

The worse things get for us, the worse they feel, the more important it is that we reaffirm who we are. That we keep giving away our time and money, yes, to Israel and to Jewish causes, but also to people in need in general. The worse things feel, the more important it is that we stand up not only for our own religious freedom, but for everyone's. The worse things feel, the more important it is that we actively and vocally participate in the intellectual discourse of this country, the political discourse, the development of new technology, and in the artistic process of writing books, essays, plays, articles, music, movies, TV shows, and more.

In a post–October 7 world, our place in this country feels more tenuous than ever. It also feels more profound. Both are probably true. And, to me, that's why doubling down on our Jewish identity—on what makes us unique, what makes us special, on showing the world who we really are—matters more than it ever has.

BRADLEY TUSK is a venture capitalist, a political strategist, a philanthropist, and a writer. He is the cofounder and managing partner of Tusk Venture Partners, the world's first venture capital fund that invests solely in early stage startups in highly regulated industries, and is the founder of political consulting firm Tusk Strategies. Bradley's family foundation is funding and leading the national campaign to bring mobile voting to all U.S. elections. Tusk Philanthropies also runs and funds antihunger campaigns that have led to the creation of antihunger policies and programs (including universal school breakfast programs) in nineteen states, helping to feed nearly 13 million people.

Bradley is the author of *The Fixer: My Adventures Saving Startups from Death by Politics, Obvious in Hindsight,* and *Vote with Your Phone: Why Mobile Voting Is Our Final Shot at Saving Democracy*; writes a column for the New York *Daily News*; hosts a podcast called *Firewall* about the intersection of tech and politics; and is the cofounder of the Gotham Book Prize. He owns a bookstore, podcast studio, event space, and café called P&T Knitwear on Manhattan's Lower East Side. He is also an adjunct professor at Columbia Business School.

Joanna Rakoff

The Weight of History

I n Barcelona, we could not find the synagogue. We checked the address, once, twice, three times, as we navigated the narrow medieval alleys of the Jewish Quarter, but when we got there, we found nothing but a wood-framed door that appeared to lead to some sort of cellar. On our third go-round, I peered into the small, dusty window, level with my feet, which gave me just a glimpse into the room below. I could barely make out a large stone wall.

Just then, the singing started. A Hebrew prayer unfamiliar to me, in a tune equally foreign, emanated faintly from the window. My husband, Keeril, and I looked at each other. Of course, the synagogue was underground, behind an unmarked door. We were in Inquisition territory. Around us, Barcelona surged with tourists, sipping cava at outdoor cafés and shopping for espadrilles, following tour guides through the winding streets.

Until that moment, Keeril and I had been among them, joyfully gazing at the Bridge of Sighs and St. Mary of the Sea.

But here at Sinagoga Mayor, the weight of Barcelona's history came crashing down on us.

"History," I suppose, is a polite way of saying the slaughter, torture, and expulsion of the Jews who had lived in this neighborhood. The Call, as the Jewish Quarter was and is still called, was settled around 400 C.E., but with traces of Jewish life going back four centuries earlier to the city's earliest days as the Roman outpost Barcino.

Jewish life was so integrated into the city and the region of Catalonia that the geographic landmark associated with it—on every postcard, in every Instagram post—known as Montjuïc, Mount Jew, was named for the ancient Jewish cemetery at its base. So integrated that Jews made up nearly 15 percent of the city's population and financed most of its ventures, its palaces, and forays into the New World.

Until they didn't. Until the beautiful byways that now make up the booming heart of Barcelona's tourist territory became the site of a massacre. In 1391, mobs stormed through wooden doors like the one in front of me, murdering every Jew in their path. In 1492, the state made things official with the Alhambra Decree, forcing those who survived to convert, or flee, or submit to death.

Of course the synagogue was underground. How could we have thought otherwise? How could we have expected a grand temple kitted out with stained-glass windows and ersatz Greek columns? How could we have been so naïve?

We live in Cambridge, Massachusetts, where Keeril serves as a humanities dean at MIT. His office in the school's iconic dome faced the school's encampment. Several months ago, I sat in a cab on Main Street, stopped by traffic, swarmed by protesters holding signs calling for the dissolvement of the state of Israel, with sounds of their chanting "from the river to the sea" filling the air. A violent nausea began to swell inside me as the cab inched forward until my fingers started to tremble, then shake. I left the cab without a word to the driver, ran onto a side street, rested my head against a cool stone building, and willed myself not to cry. I had to move forward to safety. That was the word that ran through my head: "safety."

I was supposed to be meeting Keeril at a dinner at the home of MIT's president, an innocuous event celebrating the achievements of the Institute's retiring professors. As I walked toward the river, the chanting grew louder and louder, and once I turned the corner, onto Memorial Drive, I saw that the protesters—hundreds of them—stood directly in front of my destination. The nausea rose again and I froze in the middle of the sidewalk, unable, now, to stop the tears from rushing into my eyes. As the tears fell, the protesters began to move, surging up Memorial Drive, away from the president's house, in the direction of my home.

My son, my oldest child, was in Israel on October 7, eighteen kilometers from the Gaza border. I woke up that morning, a Saturday, earlier than usual, and padded downstairs for coffee, fueled by a strange sense of unease. As I ground the coffee beans, I noticed that my phone was flashing with text after text.

"Thinking of you," they said.

"Is Coleman okay?" they asked.

"Please tell me Coleman wasn't at that music festival," they pleaded.

Before I could make sense of these missives, another came in, from Coleman himself: "I'm in a shelter. I'm completely fine." The next day, he drove back to Tel Aviv, past rows of body bags, the desert landscape abandoned and apocalyptic. But he was not fine, not exactly, and neither was I, not fine at all.

In Spain, Keeril and I returned to the small wooden door and found it just slightly open. Inside, the brilliant Mediterranean light disappeared. Once our eyes adjusted to the darkness, we saw a slender young woman with huge, haunted eyes talking quietly to a group we instantly recognized as American. Their blustering, cheerful demeanor was at grave odds with both the guide's serious tones and what she told us about the synagogue's history. Built in 400 C.E., it had held services continuously until the expulsion. So, for a thousand years.

A *thousand* years. My mind struggled to comprehend this figure.

The guide led us through an archway into a larger room: the sanctuary. It was unlike any sanctuary I'd ever seen. A sanctuary designed *not* to be a place of worship and celebration, but to protect and barricade its congregants against murderous mobs. A sanctuary designed to hide the activities conducted inside its stone walls. The small wooden bima stood in front of six wooden benches. The voices of the American tourists swirled around me, delightedly inquiring about the Jewish community in Barcelona today, about the artifacts around us, about the funding for the restoration of the synagogue. But all I could think was *a thousand years*. A thousand years of life destroyed in two swoops, with one signature. It was that easy. What decree would come next?

ON BEING JEWISH NOW

JOANNA RAKOFF is the author of the international best-selling memoir *My Salinger Year* and the bestselling novel *A Fortunate Age*, winner of the Goldberg Prize for Outstanding Debut Fiction and the *Elle* Readers' Prize. The film adaptation of *My Salinger Year*, starring Sigourney Weaver and Margaret Qualley, is currently streaming.

Rachel Levy Lesser

Proud to Be a Jewish Little Girl

When I was in first grade, a boy in my class told me that he would not sit next to me because I "celebrated Hanukkah and didn't celebrate Christmas." It got back to the first-grade teacher, who firmly and calmly told the boy—in front of me and the rest of the class—that indeed Rachel does not celebrate Christmas; she celebrates Hanukkah. She added, "I'm sure that Rachel is proud to be a Jewish little girl."

I don't remember talking about this incident at home. Perhaps I never told my parents about it? Perhaps the school didn't, either? That would not surprise me. I grew up in a Jewish home, in a Jewish family, but every single year in school I could count the number of Jewish kids in my grade on one hand, easily. I think it's fair to say that I was culturally Jewish but maybe not so much *religiously* Jewish.

We were members of a synagogue, but we called it a temple like most other Reform Jews. My dad was on the board of our temple and other Jewish organizations, as was my mom.

We attended high holiday services every year, sitting in the second row with members of our extended family, with whom we shared the major holiday meals. We became bar and bat mitzvahs. We had the Passover Seder but did not keep Passover. We had Break the Fast although I am not sure how many people in my family actually kept the fast. We did not keep kosher. We did not light Shabbat candles every Friday night. Actually, we didn't light the candles most Friday nights. My mom never made a challah. My dad never wore a tallit or a kippah.

My dad died last summer. I sat by his bedside during his last few days as he dozed in and out of consciousness. Surprisingly, he directed me on how to plan his funeral. He wanted it to be at the temple, the same one where we sat in the second row for all those years, with "the new rabbi."

"A nice guy," my dad said.

He explained the layout of the family cemetery plots, emphasizing that he should be buried next to Mom. My mom died nearly two decades earlier, but my dad and I rarely visited the plot, nor did we go to temple on the anniversary of her death. I took off the torn black ribbon pin the day after my mother's funeral, breaking the Jewish tradition; family members are supposed to wear the ribbon for one month after an immediate family member dies.

I made sure my dad's final wishes were granted. I felt unexpectedly gutted and shocked by losing him even though his eighty-two-year-old body had been failing for some time. I had thought that his death would be easier to handle than my mom's was years ago; she was so much younger.

It was not.

I felt unmoored walking around on the planet without a living parent.

I saw a therapist shortly after my dad's death; I wasn't sleeping much and I was crying, perhaps too much? I could not get the images of my dad's painful death out of my head. As I learned in therapy, my dad's death was "traumatizing." I was the one who had to make the final calls, like when to call hospice in and when to start the morphine, negating the magical thinking that I could keep my ailing dad alive—forever.

The rabbi from my own temple emailed me after reading the eulogy I'd delivered at my dad's funeral. He reminded me that while many people had parents who lived collectively far longer than mine had, they might not have experienced the love I shared with my parents.

"You are among the lucky ones," he wrote.

Those words brought me more comfort than anything else.

I started going to temple more this past year, not just for the high holidays. I found myself there the morning of October 7, 2023. My brother came with me to a small Yizkor service of remembrance commemorating the end of the holiday of Sukkot. I sat with members of my Jewish community and shared memories of lost loved ones as information came in about the atrocities of the Hamas attacks on Israel. The small temple gatherings surprisingly comforted me more than anything else.

I went to Shabbat services last summer to hear my mother's name read on the twentieth anniversary of her death.

"It only took me twenty years to show up," I told my family.

My daughter came with me. I did not ask her to, but there she was. As I held her hand, I looked around at all the other rows filled with fellow temple members: my Jewish community.

My first-grade teacher was correct. I was proud to be a Jewish little girl. Now I am proud to be a Jewish big girl, or, I suppose, a Jewish woman. I always will be.

RACHEL LEVY LESSER is an author, freelance writer, and podcast host. Her articles and essays have appeared in Huff-Post, *Glamour, Parenting,* Kveller, *Modern Loss,* and *Grown & Flown,* as well as several anthologies. She is a graduate of the University of Pennsylvania and received her MBA from the Ross School of Business at the University of Michigan. Rachel is the author of four books, including *Life's Accessories: A Memoir (and Fashion Guide),* which served as the launching pad for the podcast *Life's Accessories.* When not writing, Rachel can be found baking, practicing yoga, and knitting scarves that she wears almost every day.

Heidi Shertok

The Jewish Way

I am a terrible cook. So terrible that my teenage daughter has barred me from entering the kitchen if I even *volunteer* to chop vegetables. And my baking skills are not much better; in fact, they are arguably worse. I once made brownies that were supposed to be cookies, but the pages of the cookbook had flipped and I hadn't noticed. It was only when the pancake-like substance came out of the oven that I realized what had happened. Thankfully, my husband is an excellent cook, which is the main reason I snapped him up; a girl's gotta eat, after all.

I say this not to publicly shame myself, but to give you an idea of the miracle that is my challah. Challah is the one food that I always get right. Not only do I always get it right, but it's *good*. This, in my opinion, is even more miraculous than the splitting of the sea and the wonder of Chanukah and the victory of the Six-Day War. I imagine there are probably two or three angels in the kitchen with me when I prepare the dough, muttering under their breath and rolling

33

their eyes as they fix the mistakes that I don't even realize I'm making.

Why am I worthy of being the recipient of such a super-natural phenomenon? While I'd like to say that I'm on the same spiritual plane as our Torah heroines, sadly, that's not the case. Had I been Sarah, for example, I'd have taken a sword to certain male parts of Abraham before letting him sleep with another woman, let alone my handmaid, who knew the size of my underwear. And, unlike Rebecca, if a strange man tried to lure me back to his neck of the woods by prom-ising me a husband, I'd make a run for it. As for Rachel, I would've simply told my sister Leah, "Sorry, sucks to be you," and then gone ahead and married the man I loved. (Not that I'm a total monster—I'd bring her back presents from our honeymoon, such as a pretty nose ring or the latest model of camel.)

Admittedly, I'm not righteous. But the woman I'm named after was.

Known to family and friends as "Chayka," my maternal great-grandmother was born and raised in Lithuania. Like me, she was small in stature, less than five feet, but unlike me, she didn't order six-inch stilettos off the internet and then whine that her feet hurt. No, Chayka was too sensible for that. By all accounts, she was a stern, no-nonsense type of person who wasn't particularly demonstrative and rarely smiled, but she dedicated her life to helping others, serving the Jews within her community, and even sending food to children in Africa.

Baking was *her thing*. Not only did she tirelessly bake for fundraisers, but what little money she had she gave away to charity. And on November 20, 1999, she was posthumously awarded for being one of the founders and mentors of the Twin Cities Women's Chevra Kadisha. In that respect, at least, I have followed in her footsteps, and would, I hope, make her proud.

Chayka was the very definition of the Jewish spirit. Having seen the worst in humanity as a child in Lithuania, acts of terror that swept through her ghetto as easily as a bad rainstorm, she must've collected enough trauma to fill a psych ward. The vandalism of Jewish businesses, the beatings, the murder, the sexual violence: scenes straight out of the antisemitic playbook. And yet, much like challah dough, she rose above it, *despite it all*. She came to a new country not knowing a soul or understanding the language, and settled in a city that was still far from being Jew-friendly (not to mention the terrible weather—sorry, Minneapolis, but you know it's true). Chayka, like generations of Jews before her and since, took the dirt and grime of her past and transformed it into magnificent seeds of humanity.

Because that is the Jewish way.

I like to think that while my challah is rising, she has a little something to do with it.

HEIDI SHERTOK is a romance author, a breast cancer survivor, and a Jewish activist. She is a founding member of Artists Against Antisemitism, the Facebook group Jewish Women Talk About Romance Books, and the Jewish Joy Book Club. When she isn't writing or arguing with bots on social media, she can be found talking to herself while admiring other people's gardens.

Dara Levan

We Show Up

My phone buzzed as the plane landed and screeched to a halt. Multiple text messages from family members pinged on my phone, rapid-fire. No, no, no. I must be misreading the horrifying words, I thought.

"He died in battle."

"We wanted to make sure you knew."

"Life will never be the same."

I clutched my stomach, literally doubled over, and burst into sobs. Shocked, saddened, sickened. The cold metal seatbelt buckle dug into my belly.

My little cousin died serving his country just four weeks into the war. He was twenty-two years old. The same age as my son. Tears drenched my cheeks. My hand trembled as I passed the phone to my husband. How could this happen?

I felt helpless thousands of miles away from Israel. I wished the oxygen mask would drop down to provide air; I couldn't breathe. I'd had a similar feeling recently, as part of the global Jewish community, when the first rocket fired. When one of us is hurting, we all feel it.

In my airline seat, I felt frozen with grief, fear, and total devastation. It was already awful. I didn't think it could get worse. My son was studying abroad. My daughter had started her first year of college. All I wanted was for my babies to be back in the nest within our four safe walls. How would my family move forward? Why was my cousin taken so young, this sweet, gentle soul? So many questions. But no answers.

A few days later, my husband called a friend, Haggai, in Israel to check in. Haggai had sons who hadn't—yet—been called to serve. He shared raw details of what life was like in the Holy Land. Israelis don't let fear stop their daily lives. I've always admired how they trust that everything will work out. And that life must go on, no matter what.

"This time, though, feels different," Haggai said.

Unlike in previous years when there was a threat, on October 7, the country was completely caught off guard. I could feel and hear the trauma they were all experiencing in Haggai's voice.

When Haggai heard about my cousin, he immediately asked questions.

What unit did he serve in?

Where do the parents live?

When did it happen?

His compassion and kindness totally disarmed me. And then he said something to my husband that I honestly didn't believe.

"I'm going to the shiva. Please tell me the names of Dara's cousins, her aunt and uncle, and if you'd like me to say something specific to them," Haggai said.

His caring gesture made me cry, again. But I didn't think he'd actually *go*.

He went.

The next night, my phone dinged on WhatsApp. Photos of my little cousin popped up on the screen. I scrolled further and saw Haggai had also sent sketches of my cousin's amazing artwork that was displayed in the home. I saw images of people I didn't recognize gathered near a table and yet they felt familiar. Members of my tribe.

"Shalom, Dara. I went to the house and spoke with your cousin's mother," Haggai wrote. "I told her I was there on behalf of you and your American family. I went in uniform and paid my respects. I told them you are sending love from your home."

I had to reread the messages multiple times.

"They live in an area that's hard to get to right now," Haggai added. "But I was able to figure it out."

That's what Jews do. We move forward. We support each other. We show up.

Haggai didn't know me. I'd never spoken to him in my life. He had only met my husband at a professional organization. And yet he helped me mourn. I didn't know how to reply. How do you properly thank someone for such kindness?

"Can I call you?" I wrote back. "Or else I'll end up writing you a mini novel."

A sturdy baritone voice answered the phone.

"Shalom," he said. One small word with so much meaning.

I answered him in Hebrew. "Todah Rabah" felt stronger than a simple "thank you."

He shared more details about my family that he'd learned after spending time with them. How *loved* my cousin was and always would be. How *talented* he was in both visual and martial arts. I wiped away the tears that trickled down my cheeks. I thought about my own kids giggling when they'd tried to communicate with their cousins during our last visit to Israel. The cousins had apparently taught my kids how to curse in Hebrew.

"I don't even know how to thank you. Seriously," I sputtered.

There are no strangers in Judaism.

I remembered the words another cousin had shared, a wise rabbi, when I got married. He said, "We must always celebrate and move forward."

The world will never be the same for my family and for our community. May my young cousin's memory be a blessing. May his legacy inspire us all to live with joy. And may one acquaintance's act of kindness inspire all of us to do the same.

DARA LEVAN is an author, podcaster, and the founder of Every Soul Has a Story. What began as a weekly blog has expanded to include a podcast, an inclusive space in which she interviews guests from around the globe. Her debut novel, *It Could Be Worse*, came out in 2024. She is a graduate of Indiana University with a B.A. in English and certificate in journalism. Dara earned her M.S. in communication sciences and disorders at Nova Southeastern University. Dara is a member of the Authors Guild, the Women's Fiction Writers Association, and the Women's National Book Association, and a founding member of Artists Against Antisemitism. Dara's husband and two children are her greatest sources of inspiration. When she's not writing in South Florida, you'll find Dara with her family and fur babies, traveling, reading, and talking to strangers who become friends.

Harper Kincaid

The Revolutionary Act of Jewish Joy

There's who we were before October 7 and who we are now. Since then, I've been sleepwalking through a version of the Upside Down I could never have imagined. Just like in *Stranger Things*, the surface level is eerily status quo, carrying on in the relative safety and privilege of being Americans. There are exceptions: Jewish college students at elite schools, the observant wearing religious garb walking down the street, or even the secular Jews attending a peaceful rally to bring attention to the hostages while holding an Israeli flag. Meanwhile, not in small towns like the fictional Hawkins, Indiana, but in urban centers nationwide, a virus of hate mutates, donning revisionist labels for an ancient sickness that won't die.

Let's be honest: compared to our ancestors and modern-day Israeli citizens, Jewish Americans know we've had the easier end of the deal. We've never had the need for bomb shelters at public venues or safe rooms in our homes. We're not sending our young adults off for mandatory military service or counting on our fingers and toes the names of people we lost to wars that never should have started.

But after visiting Israel four times, I also understand that while we've had it easier, that doesn't mean we've had it better.

I've never heard of observant Israelis having to reassure new employers that honoring Shabbat won't interfere with their work obligations like one of my friends had to, only to be *reassured* with "I went to Tulane *Jew*niversity; I get it." Israelis aren't subjected to *compliments* telling them they "don't look Jewish," because in Israel Jews come in more varieties than the twenty-four Crayola skin tone pack. We're not a race, but an ethno-religion. That doesn't mean there isn't racism and all the other -isms that plague the human condition; Israel is a parliamentary democracy, not a utopia.

There have been so many times I'd click with someone, only to see the warmth drain from their faces, hardening into a familiar ugliness, when they found out I was a Jew, even though I certainly wasn't hiding it. These incidents aren't constant, but they happen enough that I've fine-tuned a version of code-switching used to divulge, instead of assimilating. I throw out something Jewish-y in the first five minutes of conversation. An example: "Ugh you're right. Partners are so hard to shop for. Every Chanukah I'm at a complete loss of what to get mine."

Israelis don't have the luxury of worrying about micro-aggressions, because they've been too busy trying to keep their citizens of all races, ethnicities, and faiths *alive*. Israelis, like Americans, are not a monolith, but each time I've visited over the last twenty years, I've marveled at how, when the sirens blared, every car stopped on the highway. People stood still on sidewalks, bustling seconds before. This is how they honor the dead.

Those same streets will be blocked off soon enough to celebrate ancient harvests and wedding feasts and independence days. Their tables are laden with fragrant spices, wines, and olives cultivated on the same land as our biblical ancestors. We are thousands of years old, and yet, many Israelis live more wholly in the present. Jewish joy is our people's birthright, but the Israelis I've met embody life in a way that can be experienced only by those who are familiar with death.

Whether it's the *sabras* who have lived there for generations or the fresh-off-the-El-Al flight *olim*, Israelis understand, for the Jewish diaspora, Israel is our backup date to the Homecoming dance. With the enactment of the Law of Return by the Knesset on July 5, 1950, many Jewish Americans celebrated an alternative, belated Independence Day, letting out a collective breath we didn't know we were holding. We had protection granted by a sovereign nation, just in case the "never again" returned. History doesn't repeat, but it always rhymes.

October 7 was like a nuclear blast without warning. The twenty-four-hour news cycle in the ensuing months was a fallout I couldn't peel myself away from, no matter how sick it made me. My heart broke for the families of the hostages, for the murdered music lovers, kibbutzniks, and, later, for the Palestinian children, all while thanking G-d my daughters were safe. The guilt of that relief remains, like pebbles in my shoe with the hard-press of cold stone under my feet, both a penance and a prayer with every step.

In the late 1970s, I attended a Hebrew day school, where I experienced my share of Jewish joy. Yet every year the staff commemorated *Yom HaShoah,* Holocaust Remembrance Day, by plastering photos from concentration camps along the walls. Piles of bodies. Tattooed arms. Emaciated survivors somehow standing. I was seven years old.

"This is what happens when you get too comfortable," we were told. "This is what happens when you let your guard down. Don't look at the Christmas tree. Don't date the Gentiles. Never forget."

I used to go to sleep with pillows over my head, burrowing under blankets, pretending I was hiding from the Nazis. How long could I hold my breath until my *Kapo* lungs would give out, gasping for air, revealing my hiding place? I'm fifty-four years old and sometimes it's the only way I can fall asleep. But now I'm deep underground, in a tunnel with no air and little food. The Upside Down is everywhere.

Months ago, I was sitting with friends, the only Jew among them. What was happening on college campuses, in big cities, and in Israel came up in conversation and everyone looked my way. I made an inappropriate, dark joke, typical of my humor, asking which one of them would hide my family if it came to that. I couldn't help but make a mental note of who said they would and who hesitated. Among my Jewish friends, we hold space for shared pain, processing the lack of support from other groups we thought were allies, reading off hateful DMs from fellow authors, for not condemning Israel. For being Zionists.

It dawned on me that I had a decision to make: Do I take my broken heart and put it back together with something hard or something more expansive? My anger and grief are two dark angels wrestling each other through the night, both taking their turn of brief dominion and respite. But if you've ever put two mirrors in front of each other, they just reflect the same image back for infinity. To mimic the vitriol being thrown at us only feeds the Upside Down under our feet, the soil from which the future will feed.

I choose the fullness and salvation of Jewish joy.

I started wearing a Star of David and lighting Shabbat candles on Friday nights. I joined a Jewish therapists' peer support group and became a founding member of Artists Against Antisemitism. And even though the part of my brain that calculates math and learns other languages remains the size of a shriveled-up raisin, I downloaded an app and practiced Hebrew. I reply to every nasty DM with an invitation for open dialogue. One replied.

I'm going to keep lighting my Shabbat candles, writing, and focusing on what brings me closer to my people. My Jewish identity has never been solely a reactive impulse against antisemitism. Our center will hold, for we are grounded in joy, family, and the sanctity of life. Oh, and lots of food. There are seats at my table for anyone who wants to join.

HARPER KINCAID is a woman with the heart of a revolutionary, the mind of a pragmatist, and the inappropriate humor of your tipsy best friend. She is a bestselling author of romance, mysteries, and creative nonfiction essays, as well as a licensed clinical psychotherapist specializing in neurodivergent creatives. When not writing, she is making art, listening to lo-fi on vinyl, fangirling theater, and otherwise being grateful for her life with her husband, two grown daughters, and two spoiled dogs.

Alix Strauss

Love in the Unlikeliest of Places

A couple grips hands. A bouquet of fresh flowers rests in her arms, while a lone flower resides in his lapel. Their faces are bright and filled with joyful pride.

A second pair looks thoughtfully and lovingly into each other's eyes.

A third, overcome with emotion, weeps throughout their ceremony.

Each of the forty photos depicting eleven couples' weddings are visually rich with history and texture. They purposely capture the people, along with a devoted, connective feeling, matched by the historic, important period in which they happened. Most shockingly, the photos are optimistic, especially since they were taken during and shortly after the Holocaust, at a time when more than 6 million Jewish people were being eradicated by the Nazis.

These stories are recounted and shared in an exhibit titled "Weddings During the Holocaust," which is one of seventy online exhibitions conceived, curated, and produced by Yad Vashem, the World Holocaust Remembrance Center, Israel's largest Holocaust memorial and museum.

As a longtime trend and pop culture journalist (over the past twenty-five years I've written more than 1,500 articles), it's not unusual for me to focus on love, relationships, and— predominantly for the *New York Times*—weddings. I've covered hundreds of weddings centered on lost love, found love, hidden love, forbidden love, mistaken love, brokenhearted love, toxic love, fairy-tale love, I'll-do-anything-to-keep-you love, and, of course, good-old-fashioned rom-com love. So, when a reader contacted me about this exhibit and asked me to consider covering it, I was intrigued. Then I became awestruck by the obvious and ironically heartbreaking-yet-hopeful juxtaposition: love found in the ashes of lives that were destroyed.

Until researching this exhibit, it hadn't occurred to me that weddings would even have been possible during this horrific period in history: that finding love, having love, let alone falling in love, would be obtainable while people were desperately trying to survive.

But these couples didn't just survive; they rebuilt. They created new homes and communities. They had children. They carried on. They endured, and thus told the story of what happened. They wanted to be heard, understood, and accepted. That's part of what makes these people special. It's part of what it means to be Jewish.

As Jews, the telling of our history, events, and happenings is part of what weaves our religion and our community together. It's a shared, intricate tapestry of unbreakable voices and accounts forever stitched together by lineage and faith. We have learned to hold on to the past because it grounds us, unifies us, gives us understanding and clarity. The greatest concern now is that many of these survivors, due to age and health concerns, will not be here much longer to personally share their knowledge. And in that, there is an undeniable alert for me: the responsibility to share their voices and to tell their stories when they no longer can.

Though the Holocaust happened decades ago, I'm linked to these brides and grooms by ancestry and epigenetics. The exhibit is about mourning for something I will never truly understand. It's about unacceptable loss and cruelty. It's about hope. And, in many ways, it's about love, the greatest of unifiers. Regardless of our faith or beliefs, we all want and deserve love. Even during the Holocaust.

ALIX STRAUSS is a trend, culture, and lifestyle journalist; an award-winning, four-time published author; a speaker; and a frequent contributor to the *New York Times*. She has been a featured lifestyle, travel, and trend writer on national morning and talk shows, including on ABC, CBS, CNN, and the *Today* show. Her books include *The Joy of Funerals, Based Upon Availability*, and *Death Becomes Them: Unearthing the Suicides of the Brilliant, the Famous & the Notorious*. She is also the editor of *Have I Got a Guy for You*, an anthology of mother-coordinated dating horror stories. Her work has been optioned for several TV and film projects. *The Joy of Funerals* is in early development with A24 for series adaptation. Alix lectures extensively and has been a keynote speaker, moderator, or panelist at more than two hundred conferences, symposiums, seminars, and summits. She lives in New York.

PART TWO

You Have to Laugh

Amy Ephron

I Once Had a Fight with a Mohel

I once had a fight with a mohel. When my son Ethan was born, my first husband, Sasha, who is Israeli, insisted, despite my and our pediatrician's hesitation, that we hire a mohel.

The mohel was very old and very short and wore a very small yarmulke that had gold stitching. He walked slowly up the front steps to our Spanish-style house with its large living room that was filled with guests. He hesitated in the entryway to have a talk with me.

"What's your Hebrew name?" he asked me.

"My name is Amy," I answered.

"No. What is your *Hebrew* name?"

"I don't have one," I said. "My name is Amy."

"You have to have a Hebrew name," he said, implying that I couldn't take part in the ceremony unless I had one.

I shook my head.

"How do you feel about Hannah?" he asked.

"Not good," I answered.

It escalated from there. Me insisting my name was Amy. I even tried to pull rank.

"My ancestor is in the Bible," I told him forcefully. "Ephron. He was a Hittite. He owned a graveyard. In Genesis." I softened my voice. "He may not have been a very nice guy, but lately there's been research to dispute that. We're four girls, so we may be the end of the line or one line anyway, but he's there. Direct relative."

No win.

Me insisting again that my name is Amy. Him now saying I couldn't take part in the ceremony unless I had a Hebrew name.

I looked over at Sasha, hoping he would intercede.

No luck.

"My name is Amy," I screamed.

I stormed up the stairs with my best friend Holly and hid in our bedroom. Once the door was shut, Holly and I burst into uncontrollable laughter, the kind of laughter you break into when something has gone terribly wrong. Secretly, I was quite happy to miss Ethan's penis-cutting procedure. We did not go back downstairs until we watched, from the window, the mohel totter down the outdoor steps.

Twenty-Four Years Later

My oldest daughter, Maia, was getting married on the rooftop of the London Hotel in L.A. Maia and Matt both looked fabulous. Picture-perfect. Blissful. But they were being married by a rabbi who was much more conservative and religious than I expected. He spent a lot of time talking about religion. I should not have been surprised, as I had been apprised that only men were allowed to sign their ketubah. (The ketubah is a formal Jewish wedding contract.) The only signers would be my first husband (my ex), Sasha, and Matt's father, Mark.

We walked from the roof to a meeting room in the hotel. On the outside walkway at the ground level, I pulled Sasha back.

"Now you're going to make it up to me for the mohel," I said.

Sasha gave me one of those looks, like, *What is she up to now?*

"Here's the thing," I said. "You're the only one in that room who speaks Hebrew besides that rabbi."

He nodded.

"So you're going to tell him, in Hebrew, in that forceful Israeli voice you use sometimes, that I'm going to sign the ketubah, too. He'll believe you because you're Israeli and he'll instantly agree."

I put my hand on my hip for emphasis and somehow got Sasha to say okay. The rules about ketubahs are wiggly, anyway. Some people say family members aren't supposed to sign. In this case, the rabbi had said it was only men.

We sat down at a conference table in a windowless room in the lower level of the hotel, strangely religious (or mafialike, if you wish), and Sasha, as instructed, burst into Hebrew without letting the rabbi get a word in until he was done.

The rabbi blinked, nodded, nodded again, and said in English, "Okay." *Okay* is one of those words that seems to have crossed over from English to Hebrew.

Someone in the room asked what had just gone on.

The rabbi answered, "Amy, Maia's mother, is going to sign the ketubah, too."

Matt, to his credit, chimed in, without missing a beat, "If Amy's going to sign the ketubah, I want my mom, Rhonda, to sign it, too."

The rabbi did not ask either of us if we had a Hebrew name.

AMY EPHRON is a bestselling author. She has three children and a second husband.

Nicola Kraus

My Perimenopausal Bat Mitzvah

I n the summer of 2023, my friend Caroline texted me:
"This coming fall, East End Temple is offering Adult
Hebrew for the first time."

"So only the dirty words?" I texted back.

"Haha. Will you do it with me?"

I was stunned. My husband and I celebrated Passover at her
house and Caroline always seemed so proficient in Hebrew
that I'd assumed she was already . . . fluent? Is that a thing?

"You don't speak Hebrew?" I asked.

"I was never bat mitzvahed," she replied. "It was more for
the boys then."

I thought back to my own experience in the late 1980s.
I'd assumed the reason why very few girls in my circles had
enjoyed the combination rite of passage and blowout party
had something to do with the pervasive WASPiness of the
Upper East Side. But maybe it was more gendered than that.

"So?" she texted. "Will you?"

I contemplated the undertaking for a second. My husband had gone back to school full-time, so I was doubling

up on work to avoid completely depleting our savings, plus lead-parenting while he attended long days of classes and tackled his coursework. Yes, taking Hebrew had been on my Things I Really Need to Do Ideally After My Daughter Leaves for College and I Have More Bandwidth list. Right up there with pickleball and finally going to Australia. Was this really the time to add a meatball on my plate?

Still, the opportunity to have a Hebrew buddy was too good to pass up. "YES! Let's do it."

On a warm September evening, I took two trains into Manhattan. I had attended a bar and bat mitzvah at East End Temple and volunteered at their monthly Food for Families events for City Harvest, but I was not, technically, or in any other way, a member of the congregation. I had, however, taken Introduction to Judaism with the rabbi over Zoom during the pandemic and adored his ability to embrace nuance and wrestle with contradiction. If I was going to "belong" anywhere, it would be here.

On the fourth floor we waited patiently as the tweens beginning their bar and bat mitzvah slogs filed out, backpacks in tow. Then fifteen of us took our seats and our instructor, Elyssa, asked us to go around the horseshoe, introduce ourselves, and tell the group what had brought us here.

I had hoped that there might be a couple young women in their twenties converting to Judaism who might be as lost as I was. But no. Contrary to my expectation, everyone else was an active member of the temple. One person even sat on the board. But either they had never been bat mitzvahed or the men felt that they had forgotten everything since and wanted a refresher.

When my turn came I had no idea how to artfully present my situation, so I just spat it out: "I was raised Episcopalian by Jews." There was politely controlled flinching.

I explained, "Three of my great-grandparents were killed in the camps. My grandparents fled to London and New York, changed their names, and never spoke about Judaism or the Holocaust ever again. I was christened at St. James, sent to Episcopalian schools, and it wasn't until I studied the Holocaust in eighth grade that I connected the stories of fleeing grandparents with being Jewish. Anyway, I've now been back to the Czech Republic for ceremonies to honor not only my relatives but the members of their extended community who were killed. And I want to try to reconnect to this lost part of my heritage."

I hoped that was enough to justify my presence.

Elyssa went on to explain that over the next twenty-six weeks we would learn the Hebrew alphabet and then, if we wanted to continue, we could come back in year two to prepare for a group b'nai mitzvah where we would be called to the torah.

"I want a dance squad," Caroline whispered to me.

"A slideshow," I whispered back.

Quickly our b'nai mitzvah theme came into focus: Ice Sculptures; Hot Flashes. I was getting excited.

Then we opened our lesson books and turned to page one. That was when it hit me. Hebrew . . . was in Hebrew.

As the lines and squiggles swirled around the page, I realized to my exhausted horror that there would be no bopping around with a Walkman listening to a prerecorded Torah portion that I could learn phonetically. I was going to be asking my wrung-out, estrogen-depleted, mildly dyslexic brain to memorize an entirely new system of symbols—in a written system that will yank away the vowels at some point like a parent deciding training-wheels days are over.

"Hear us out," Caroline and I would say week after week as we arrived in what should have been our dinner hour, now in the dark, now in snow, now during weather that had driven people indoors and transformed my subway platforms into crisis centers. "What about 9 a.m. Hebrew?"

There were no takers.

But I persevered. By December I was able to nudge my husband during the film *Maestro* and say, "Harvard! His sweatshirt says Harvard!" And by May I could start to read some prayers, even if I lacked childhood memories of them.

I persevered because after the October 7 attack it became so clear that all of it—even the headache—was a privilege. It was a privilege that the carriers of this language had survived. It was a privilege to study it in safety. It was a privilege to be in community with other people good-humoredly humbling ourselves to something bigger than ourselves. And it was a privilege to belong. Or to be studying toward belonging.

One year later and I'm preparing for the next raft of challenges—canting, memorization, losing vowels. But this time I no longer feel like an interloper. At fifty, I feel like I'm home.

NICOLA KRAUS is a #1 *New York Times* bestselling author with more than 6 million copies in print in thirty-two languages. Her novel with Emma McLaughlin, *The Nanny Diaries*, was an international #1 bestseller. In addition to publishing nine more novels with Emma McLaughlin, in 2015 Nicola cofounded the creative consulting firm The Finished Thought, which helps the next generation of aspiring authors find their voice. Through her work there she has collaborated on several *New York Times* nonfiction bestsellers. Her first solo novel, *The Best We Could Hope For,* comes out in 2025.

Mark Feuerstein

Electric Jew-ga-loo!

I win every dance contest in seventh grade. It's 1984. The movie *Breakin'* has just come out. I am the Turbo of the Upper East Side. Larry Ozone is the "party catalyst" for every bar mitzvah, and on Saturday nights, whether at Temple Emanuel or the Plaza Hotel, good ole Larry taps out kid after kid until it's just me popping and locking my way to victory. Breakdancing is more of an expression of who I am at that time than either my Haftorah portion or my speech reflect. (Okay, let's face it, my dad had a *significant* hand in writing my speech. No thirteen-year-old knows the word "perspicacious.") But breakdancing is my thang, genuine self-expression, and I'm so grateful that our religion provides such a wide container into which I can celebrate my love of street dance.

At the center of every table are papier-mâché statues of Michael Jackson, whose "Billie Jean" number at the twenty-fifth Motown anniversary knocked me out. I watched it a thousand times on my VCR. My parents miraculously corral five incredible breakdancers to flatten their cardboard on the parquet floor of the ballroom at Park East Synagogue. Sporting my "tap-dance kid" T-shirt and Girbaud parachute pants, I'm popping and locking with this insane crew right next to my grandparents, Baruch and Jean Seigel, a perfect juxtaposition. Simcha and Chutzpah mingle with my friends and family on that fateful night.

It doesn't necessarily make me a man so much as solidify my identity as an "extra," over-the-top showman. It's not about conspicuous consumption; it's about breakin', it's about slipping on my black gloves with the fingers cut off and my Pumas with the black-and-white checked laces and hitting the floor. Every kid gets a T-shirt at the end of the night that reads "Push it to pop it. Pop it to rock it. BREAK IT TO MAKE IT!" Aw, yeah! This tagline, stolen from *Breakin'* (not to be confused with *Breakin' 2: Electric Boogaloo*), says it all and I love that a ritual where we read from sacred texts can also include *that* sacred message.

Now I'm a dad, and it comes time for my kids' b'nai mitzvah. Frisco and Addie's personalities shine through in their speeches about the binding of Isaac, and their swag reads FUN AF. (My dad still thinks "AF" stands for "Addie" and "Frisco.")

Satisfied that their party was as reflective of who they are as mine was of me, I slip in a request that the party catalysts include a breakdancer. Jason had been part of an OG breakin' crew in Crenshaw in the eighties. He was the real deal. And when the MC turns to me mid-party and says, "You good to break-battle against J right now?" I thought he was joking. Surely, in break-battling, I'd break my neck. Then again, how could I turn down the opportunity, some thirty-two years later, to win my last dance contest of all time?

"Hell, yeah, I'm good. Let's DO THIS!"

The MC announces the break-off and the kids start chanting my name: "Mark, Mark, Mark!" I was basically a Jewish version of "Frank the Tank" from *Old School*, but instead of a bunch of frat guys cheering, it's one hundred fifty middle school kids.

This was too much, I thought. My son and daughter will rip my head off for embarrassing them on their big night. But then I thought of Rabbi Hillel's famous words: "If not now . . . when?" and suddenly, like all respectable fifty-year-old dads, I'm a robot, karate-chopping up and down, sending that electric pulse out with one hand and then catching it with the other.

Once I've aggressively moonwalked up to Jason and maturely mimed taking out his brain and stomping on it, the MC sends it back to J, who proceeds to wipe the floor with me: spinning on his head and doing the windmill.

Well, that was fun, I thought. *All's well that ends well.*

But then the MC sends it to me AGAIN! Wait, what? I'm done. Frank's got nuthin' left in the tank. But actors gotta act and dancers gotta dance, so I dig deep, do some solid floor work, and kick my feet around randomly in a circle. And then . . . that's right, folks, I go for it, this fifty-year-old risks splitting open his chin and does THE WORM! Crowd goes wild. The Kid is BACK! And believe it or not, the MC dubs ME the winner of the Break-dance Battle!!! (I'm certain it has *nothing* to do with the fact that I'm paying him.)

Sure, this is the story of an attention-monger who pathetically tried to steal some of his former glory as a child breakdancer at his kids' b'nai mitzvah and wound up needing back surgery that summer. But it's *also* a story about Jewish joy and the ways in which our traditions, from seders, to weddings, to bar mitzvahs, allow us to "make it our own." Judaism celebrates difference and idiosyncrasy, and that is something I cherish.

MARK FEUERSTEIN has worked consistently in Hollywood since the late nineties. In addition to being a writer and a director, Mark is best known as an actor, specifically for his starring role in the USA Network series *Royal Pains.* His other television credits include *The West Wing, Sex and the City, Prison Break,* and *The Baby-Sitters Club.* Some of his feature credits include *What Women Want, In Her Shoes,* and *Practical Magic.* Mark grew up in New York, graduated from Princeton University, and won a Fulbright Scholarship, which took him to the London Academy of Music and Dramatic Art. Mark's most recent projects are *Hotel Cocaine* on MGM+ and *Lady in the Lake* on Apple+. He lives in Los Angeles with his wife and three precious children.

Bess Kalb

A Short and Private Thing About Writing About Being Jewish

I met a person on my book tour who said my writing since October 7 has meant a lot to her and she thanked me a few times, slowly and pointedly. I felt queasy, as if I'd been caught. I turned red and started to sweat. I felt odd accepting this about my writing because so much of it (*except this!*) feels like a lie (*or is it?*).

When I write about politics, I get to choose my words carefully and see them against a gleaming white screen, and then edit them. I can take a shower and come back to the screen and delete entire paragraphs with a practiced keystroke. I can rid the screen of the inflammatory and emotional and instinctive and unprocessed garbage ideas that I have. Garbage generated by the same brain that produced the writing that made it to your screen in a tidy and digestible way.

There is the writing I capture in a screenshot and crop to fit your screen, and there is the writing I do in WhatsApp texts to my friends. There is the barely coherent grunting I do with my cousin. There is the ranting I do with (*at*) my husband after the kids go to bed.

There is no perfect take about antisemitism, and I certainly don't have it. There are people who know more and have seen more than I have. There is suffering beyond the knee-jerk projections I have about my perfectly safe kid.

If my writing has been meaningful to you, I'm glad. But know that I don't remember what I wrote in a flash of processing, because I've thought the opposite of everything all at once.

I've come back around to the most basic truth of all this: There are worse things happening right now than antisemitism. There is a fear of history that can turn blinding. There is a fear of history that leads to the justification of brutality. But there is also the look in my grandma's eyes. That she can so easily remember the chants of the kids who sang a song about her killing Christ and drinking the blood of Christian babies while her relatives were gassed alive.

All of it is horrible and the pain is real.

This is a time when there is so much we cannot say, and so much we can't help but feel and fear, so thank you for bearing with me while I say the most polished parts of that. I'm grateful you've listened. What I'm saying is: Thank you.

BESS KALB is an Emmy-nominated comedy writer and the bestselling author of *Nobody Will Tell You This but Me*, a *New York Times* Editors' Choice. She wrote for eight years on *Jimmy Kimmel Live!*. She received a WGA Award in 2016. She has written for the Emmy Awards, the Oscars, and the 2020 DNC. She is the head writer and executive producer of Amazon Prime's *Yearly Departed*. Her book is currently being adapted into a feature film by Sight Unseen Pictures.

David K. Israel

Covenant

I n the wet, sticky beginning of October 2023, I found myself wading through the soggy aftermath of a breakup so disastrous it felt almost biblical. Three months had passed since the initial explosion, yet the debris still cut my feet. I believed I'd reached bedrock, the very nadir, but it turned out I was merely grazing the surface of the bottom. Then October 7 burst forth, uninvited, and would forever be more than just a date on the calendar.

Much like 9/11, 10/7 became another one of those grim signposts: the kind that etches itself into your brain, ensuring you'll never forget what you were doing (rehearsing a new ballet score I was going to play live) or who you were with (New York Theater Ballet folk) when the news first shattered the air.

Over the next many months, things would deteriorate even more than I thought possible—not just for the situation in Israel and Gaza, but for me, personally. Anti-Trump and anti-MAGA sentiments on women's dating profiles (yes, I was trying to get back out there) were quickly replaced with language like: "Swipe left if you're a Zionist!" The women on the apps, clueless to the traumatizing antisemitism I'd experienced growing up in a small town in South Jersey, were merely trying to filter out potential bad matches—just as they might want to do with men who had children still in diapers, lived more than twenty-five miles outside their radius, or had unwelcome facial hair. But for me, they just as well might have written: NO KIKES!

To help stay afloat during this hellish, confusing sea change, in the Jewish tradition, I turned to comedy. The following was the result, a reimagined Ten Commandments:

Biblical scholars have long recognized the language of the Ten Commandments as different from the rest of the writings found in the Old Testament. Similar in style to standard legal contracts of the era, the Ten Commandments were penned by Hebrew scribes to reflect the seriousness with which their people took their contract with their God.

Last week, archaeologists working in the caves near Qumran, where the Dead Sea Scrolls were found some three quarters of a century ago, discovered a redlined re-draft of the contract. By comparing this early version of the Covenant to the one that ultimately made its way into Exodus, scholars now surmise the Israelites not only wrestled with their God on many of the issues, but most likely had lawyers present.

A partial translation:

This Covenant ("Covenant") is entered into as of this day, the first day of the third month after the Exodus from Egypt, between Yahweh (hereinafter referred to as "Party of the First Part," and legally defined as "The Lord, God") and the People of Israel (hereinafter referred to as "Party of the Second Part," and legally defined as "The Chosen People").

Whereas the Party of the First Part has outlined a set of laws, whereby the Party of the Second Part must adhere.

And whereas the period of the Covenant shall last for all of Eternity (or one billion trillion years, whichever comes first), commencing as of the date hereof ("Term").

NOW, THEREFORE, IT IS AGREED BY AND BETWEEN THE PARTIES HERETO:

1. The Party of the Second Part hereby waives the right to enter into any Covenant with another God, including, but not limited to: Dharmic deities, pantheistic and henotheistic Gods, or any God that would be so frivolous as to play dice with the universe.

2. The Party of the Second Part may not produce or distribute a sculpted image, idol, or icon, in whole or in part, of anything that is in heaven above, or that is on the earth beneath, or that is in the water under the earth, without engaging a consulting firm that specializes in branding or brand strategy preapproved by the Party of the First Part (e.g., Ogilvy, Landor & Fitch; see Exhibit A for complete list).

3. The Party of the Second Part shall not swear falsely by the name of the Party of the First Part except under the following two (2) proviso(s):
    i) You get to the airport and realize you left your ID at home (e.g., "Goddamn it!")
    ii) You strike your thumb with a hammer (e.g., "God-f*!@ing-damn it!")

4. *The Party of the Second Part shall remember the Sabbath day and keep it holy except under the following one (1) proviso:*

  i) There's a sale at Bergdorf's

5. *The Party of the Second Part shall honor mothers and fathers one day a year with the presentation of a greeting card (e.g., a talking strawberry proclaiming, "You're one berry, berry special mom!")*

6. *The Party of the Second Part shall not commit murder except under the following seventeen thousand and forty-one (17,041) proviso(s) [partial list only—see Exhibit B for complete list]:*

  i) To spread the word written herein

  ii) To solve a land dispute

  iii) To spread freedom and democracy

  iv) To impress Jodie Foster

7. *Whereas the Party of the First Part created the heavens and the earth in six (6) days, and rested on day seven (7) (See Genesis 2:1), the Party of the Second Part shall not commit adultery before the Seven (7)-Year Itch.*

8. *The Party of the Second Part shall not steal, burgle, loot, plagiarize, pilfer, shoplift, embezzle, rip off, blackmail, or defraud. However, stealing another's thunder is permissible, especially when with child; also: The sampling of single grapes at Stop & Shop shall not be considered theft.*

9. *The Party of the Second Part shall not bear false witness against a neighbor except under the following two (2) proviso(s):*

  i) The neighbor leaves his garbage cans at the curb for more than three (3) days after pickup

*ii) The neighbor has an annoying telephone that rings
unremittingly at all hours of the day and the night to
the tune of the Mexican hat dance*

10. *The Party of the Second Part shall not covet a neighbor's
wife, nor a maidservant, nor a manservant (especially if
the Party of the Second Part is a man; see Genesis 18:1),
nor an ox, nor an ass, nor a neighbor's house, even if
the neighbor has a Sub-Zero refrigerator, a Viking stove,
or great closet space.*

*This agreement shall constitute the entire understanding with
regard to the subject matter hereof and shall supersede and replace
any prior understanding, whether oral or carved in stone, and
may not be amended or modified. Any notices hereunder shall
be in writing and shall be given either by personal delivery, by
facsimile, or by post (postage prepaid, please) to the appropriate
party at the following address: The Burning Bush, Sinai Desert,
Egypt.*

DAVID K. ISRAEL has been telling stories with music, with
words, and through the lens for more than two decades. He
has composed commissioned scores for numerous critically
acclaimed dance pieces, working with companies such as
Paul Taylor, Twyla Tharp, and the New York City Ballet.
David has also produced, written, and sold feature films and
TV pilots. His first novel was published by Random House
and translated and sold in several countries.

Jane L. Rosen

Shopping While Jewish

I t all began in the communal dressing room at Loehmann's circa 1972. Sitting in a lone chair at seven years
old, protecting the sacred pile of yeses and maybes
that my mother and her best friend Evie Bigman told me to
guard with my life. I'd peer over the top of the discounted
designer treasures, eyes wide, mouth agape at the frenzy of
big-breasted women in giant brassieres doing their damned-
est to squeeze into ill-sized Halston dresses or Bill Blass
suits. Ladies-in-waiting, eyeing their prey, hoping for a fail.

I found it both terrifying and exhilarating. The Brits
hunted foxes in the Cotswolds. The WASPs went duck-
shooting on the shore. And the Jews? The Jews combed the
racks at Loehmann's.

My mother's other hunting ground was New York City's
Lower East Side, where we ventured a few times a year to stock
up. We visited A.W. Kaufman on Orchard Street, where I
was embarrassingly fitted for my first real bra at about fourteen. The zaftig saleswoman squeezed herself into the tiny

dressing room, barking orders at me in Yiddish while lifting and poking and measuring my chest with a tape measure as I stood, mortified, realizing that she would forever be emblazoned in my memory as the first person to feel me up. Next was Ideal Hosiery on Grand Street, where my mom would buy socks by the dozen, packed in cardboard boxes, followed by the needlepoint store, to choose a tablecloth to cross-stitch in time for the high holidays. I never understood the time my mother spent on these tablecloths, months of work wiped out in a minute by a tipsy uncle on his third glass of Manischewitz.

We would break for lunch at one of the many dairy restaurants, long, narrow, and nondescript—aside from the waiters, colorfully disgruntled old men who would drop your plate of blintzes as they passed by your table without so much as a look in your direction. It was an art form.

After lunch we would hit Guss' Pickles, on Essex (still called "Pickle Alley" then, in honor of the dozen or so pickle vendors it once housed), before our last stop: Economy Candy on Rivington for Hopjes coffee-flavored suckers and Goldenberg's Peanut Chews, which we sampled during the car ride home to Long Island.

In the summer before my senior year of college, I got a job working for my cousin at a ladies' coat company in the garment center that I returned to again for a few years after graduation. A lot of my extended family was in the *schmatta* business, and while I sometimes regret not going straight into writing, I wouldn't trade the experiences of my years on Seventh Avenue for all the borsht in Belarus. From the Lithuanian patternmaker who taught me Yiddish, to the Hasidic man from Goshen who bargained for a discount with his wife's brisket and gefilte fish, to my first introduction to the sample sale, my years there were filled with Jewish joy. But nothing came close to my experience with the buttonhole man.

Up a rickety freight elevator to the third floor of an old factory building on West Thirty-Eighth Street sat a single man in a cavernous empty room with a lone buttonhole machine—a specific sewing machine that creates buttonholes by looping the thread tightly in one direction, then the other, before slicing it down the middle. It was always silent in there, except for the *tick tick tick*ing of the machine. I would hand the man the coats (these were samples—our factory had its own buttonhole machines, but not our showroom) and watch intently as he meticulously crafted the buttonholes.

It was cool to watch, but that wasn't my only reason for staring. The man had a number tattooed on his arm, and though I was a voracious reader of Holocaust books during my typical teenage girl obsession with that era, I had never seen a survivor in person. Many in my family escaped before the Shoah. Yes, the patternmaker who taught me Yiddish hid in the Slonim woods during the entire German occupation, but I had never met someone who was in the camps.

Finally, one day, the buttonhole man caught me staring and held his forearm out for me to see.

"You can touch it," he said, in his strong Polish accent.

I ran my finger over the six digits etched into the creases and sunspots of the old man's arm as tears burned my eyes. He smiled at me, and I smiled back. He counted up the buttonholes and wrote the number down in his ledger, which I signed before gathering my coats and leaving.

I pushed my rack of samples back up Thirty-Eighth Street that day, counting my blessings. Thanking God that I had never experienced antisemitism. Thanking God that I lived in America in a time when my safety as a Jew was as indelible as the numbers on the buttonhole man's arm.

Only now, thirty years later, do I realize I was wrong.

JANE L. ROSEN is the author of five novels, *Seven Summer Weekends, Eliza Starts a Rumor, A Shoe Story, On Fire Island,* and *Nine Women, One Dress.* In her monthly column, "Cake or Pie?," she whimsically interviews her fellow authors. She is also a screenwriter and *New York Times, Tablet,* and Huff-Post contributor.

Noa Yedlin

About to Laugh

One

I'm sitting on a bench in Washington Square Park, waiting for 6 p.m.; that's the earliest you can line up to get into
the Comedy Cellar. Which leaves plenty of time for guilt.
At home, in Israel, death is everywhere, like a plague: No
one is untouched. If you're lucky, your share of death is dis-
tant, your own children are alive and not kidnapped—the
two new bizarre criteria for sanity, normalized over the past
months. Across the border, in the Gaza Strip, thousands
and thousands of Palestinians are now dead, sick, homeless.
And here I am, about to laugh. I can't even pretend it was
an accident: It's hours of waiting outside, in the rain, and if
that's not proof of intent, I don't know what is. Am I allowed
to laugh? It's one thing to laugh in Israel, an agreed-upon
laugh, one that has been carefully scrutinized from every
possible angle. But a gentile laugh, a New York City one, as
if I'm not even Jewish?

Two

This is the Jewishest I have ever felt, and I know that's not a word. It should be a word, if you ask me. A friend of mine recently told me: I will never forgive Hamas for making me sound like my grandmother. That's the way it is now: All of us bad Jews who never practice Judaism, who like to think of ourselves as citizens of the world, Westerners at heart—after all, we do watch Netflix—suddenly wear our Stars of David on our sleeves. I secretly protest: This was not the agreement. By now our Jewishness (I'm surprised to find that this *is* a word) was not supposed to be a big deal. *Really?*, a voice in me asks. *What was the agreement, then? Who exactly did you sign it with?*

Three

My husband is worried. I have a lecture scheduled at NYU and he doesn't want me to go. He reads the papers, watches the news. In his imagination, hundreds of furious antisemites burst into the room, chanting "from the river to the sea," and hold me hostage until I admit to something. I remind him that in Israel, terrorists went into people's houses, tortured, raped, and murdered them: Maybe getting the hell out of there wasn't such a bad idea. But in my heart, I know the truth. It's not that I was afraid to be in Tel Aviv; I just really wanted to be in New York. I want to pretend it's October 6. I want to be selfish.

Four

Once upon a massacre, in November 2023, my first book in the U.S. was published. I waited for so long. I worked so hard. If I pretend—just for a few days—that happiness is allowed, will I be betraying the sadness?

Five

I share my husband's concern with the professor who invited me to give the lecture. I try to make it sound like a joke. *He thinks I'm Salman Rushdie,* I tell her. She politely explains that there probably isn't much room for concern, but she could check with the Israeli consulate, just to be on the safe side.

Six

I decide to go. I prepare for my lecture as one prepares for war. I think of all the questions that I might be asked, not about my new book but about dead children in Gaza. I memorize all the English terms. I wonder if I should tell the truth, or, rather, what kind of truth I should tell. In Israel, I know who I am. I know how I sound and I know who listens. But here? I mean—there?

Seven

On the day of the lecture, there are more security guards than audience members. The Israeli consulate pitched in, NYU did their part—they all came together to make me feel like I mattered. In the absence of any disturbance, I hear myself talking about death—ironic death, literary death, like the one in my novel. I suddenly panic. If I were sitting in the audience, I realize, I would ask: *What is the meaning of ironic death when* actual *death is mocking us all?* For a moment, I lose my footing: Death is just death, simple and disgusting. Maybe some things can't be mapped by words, not without compromising their nature. The thought lures me in, until finally a question from the audience shakes me out of it. *You were talking about empathy,* someone says. I was?

Eight

When the lecture is over, I tell no one where I'm headed. It's a four-minute walk from NYU to the Comedy Cellar. There's still time, and I plan to kill it on that bench. *Kill it.* I wonder when language became such a landmine. I actually know the date.

Nine

I hear repeated calls in the distance. There's a demonstration a few hundred feet away. What are they protesting? Throughout my visit, friends and family have been texting me from Israel, wondering if I've been involved in any antisemitic incidents. They seem almost disappointed to learn that I haven't, as if I missed out on the opportunity to help them justify their cause. So here goes: I have a feeling this one is about us. I wonder if I should go and check. I want to find out that it is, and I want to find out that it isn't. I want to be reminded that people really don't care, but I also want to feel miserable and right, an irresistible combination. Let's say I go. What happens next? Is this how I'm going to die? I tell myself a little joke—*It'll be good for sales!*—but I immediately know that it won't. It's going to take a lot more than me being attacked in the middle of Washington Square Park for this book to actually sell.

Ten

On their way home, some of the protesters walk past. I try to read their signs, now held upside down. "Cease Fire Now," "Defend Gaza." I feel right anyway.

Eleven

When I finally get to the front of the line, the bouncer asks for my ID. I take out my Argentinian passport, feeling like the most devious woman around. He puts my name on a list while making small talk.

> *So, how about that new president, huh?*
> I stare at him blankly. This is one question I did not
>   prepare for.
> *Well?* he asks. *What do you make of him?*
> *I like him,* I finally say. *At last, some hope for our country.*

And for a moment there, I feel a little bit better, even though the joke's on me.

NOA YEDLIN is a bestselling Israeli author, the recipient of the Sapir Prize and the Prime Minister's Literature Award. Noa is also the creator of a two-season TV series based on her bestselling novel *Stockholm*, which was recently published in the U.S. The series was later remade around the world. She was named by *Haaretz* as one of "66 Israeli Women You Should Know."

The author is grateful to Jessica Cohen for her generous help in editing "About to Laugh."

Cara Mentzel

Moses, Mantras, and Metaphors

I was sopping wet from my hood to my Injinji toe socks. So wet that my feet were making slurping sounds through the puddles inside my trail runners. So wet I couldn't tell the difference between my sweat and my snot, a feat made even more challenging given the mosquito net cinched around my neck. Kermit, my thirty-pound backpack the color of, well, Kermit the Frog, sat on my shoulders. My husband trudged through the mud a few yards in front of me. We'd climbed more than fifteen miles that day and my right knee was giving me trouble. The pain had gone from a zero to a seven in a matter of hours. I no longer wielded my hiking poles like the badass I wanted to be, but like a post-op octogenarian with a tennis ball walker.

When I'm hiking long distances, mantras and metaphors abound, and not particularly original ones, either. I'd been marching through the forests of the Colorado Trail, repeating "core, glutes, leaves-of-three-let-them-be" since dawn. I'd contemplated how much harder it was to "take one step at a time" or "put one foot in front of the other" than well-intentioned friends would think. In fact, those are the words I interrupted as I hit yet another false peak in the storm and my inner voice exclaimed, "Moses! Moses! Moses!"

I laughed out loud at the childhood tidbit my psyche unearthed, not from the Bible, of course, but from the movie *The Ten Commandments*, a movie I'd spent far more time watching than I'd ever spent in synagogue. As vivid as the words had been, loud was the image of indefatigable sex symbol Charlton Heston, steadfast through various forms of inclement weather, bracing himself with a tall staff. Even at REI they don't make 'em like they used to. And I thought, *Here I am. All fifty years of me.*

The Colorado Trail weaves nearly five hundred miles through the Rockies from Denver to Durango. It was supposed to be a thirty-day adventure I gifted myself for my fiftieth birthday. The first day I hiked more than 16.4 miles, took a bath in the South Platte River, ate dinner out of a bag—just add hot water—and still managed to have sex with my husband. I. Was. Fierce! Nothing could stop me, except a couple more days, a deluge, and an overworked knee, apparently.

Why am I doing this? I wondered. *Why am I on this trail when I could be in bed with a cup of hot matcha and Netflix?*

In the past ten months I was coming to terms with my mortality in a way I hadn't before. I'd planned to drive from L.A. to Boulder in December. It was a drive I knew well and had done many times. My mom never likes me driving twenty hours alone—the whole "woman last seen on the shoulder of highway 70 with a flat tire" features prominently in her nightmares. This time she had other fears.

"Do you still wear the Jewish star from Grandpa Nat?" she asked.

"Yes."

"Maybe don't wear it on your trip?"

After October 7 my heritage became acutely relevant. Despite being the kind of Jew who quotes movies instead of the Torah, who earned most of her Jewish currency kissing David Allen in seventh grade and dancing to Billy Idol's "Mony Mony" at friends' bat mitzvahs, I became Jewish enough to be a target, to have an opinion people cared about. I could make a scrumptious noodle kugel (crushed pineapple and a whole stick of butter), but was I even Jewish enough to weigh in? Then two of my friends were diagnosed with aggressive forms of cancer, and another friend, very healthy and fit, died suddenly after contracting a weird strain of strep. As I approached fifty years old, I worried that midlife might not land in the middle of my life, but closer to the end. I wasn't interested in catastrophizing—there were real catastrophes taking place in the world—but I wanted to be more deliberate about what I chose to do and why.

I lead a fortunate life. I've loved the years I spent as a mother, an author, and an elementary school teacher. With my new empty nest—three grown boys have flown the coop—and perimenopause throwing me curveballs, I was gearing up for whatever came next.

On the trail I considered the ironies of perception. To hear better I say "Shhh" and ask for quiet. To see the night sky in all its bright-star, Milky Way glory, I travel farther away from the light (from light pollution). To see what's beyond the horizon, I need to back away from it. I had become so overstimulated by the world I was desensitized to my impulses and instincts.

On the trail it occurred to me that the difference between an actual deluge and a metaphorical one is that rain is just rain. It doesn't matter whether you're submerged in a puddle or a pool: Wet is wet. But if it's pouring helplessness, violence, injustice, poverty, apathy, greed, and righteousness, a sensitive person will feel every drop. Those are waters a person can sink in.

In the end, I spent five days hiking the Colorado Trail before my knee insisted I stop. I lost track of time watching an Abert's squirrel tear into a pinecone like the world's best (and last) corn on the cob. I bit into the sweetest apple I'd ever tasted and delighted over how its core reminded me of a bear den with two seedling cubs. I climbed miles imagining the gold Star of David my Grandpa Nat gave me with the garnet mounted in the center. Sometimes I pictured it nestled like a seed in the husk of his thick boxer's fist, and sometimes it twinkled, exposed in the palm of his hand. Everywhere I looked, even in my mind's eye—seeds. The potential for life. Dormant, nourishing, generative.

CARA MENTZEL's debut memoir, *Voice Lessons: A Sisters Story*, about her relationship with her superstar sister, Idina Menzel (yes, they spell their last names differently), was a Goodreads Choice Award nominee in 2017. She is coauthor of two children's books, *Loud Mouse* and *Proud Mouse*, and currently writes the blog *The Empty Next* on Substack. Cara lives in Boulder, Colorado, where she and her husband raised their Brady Bunch of boys against the beauty of the Rocky Mountains. She has a master's degree in elementary education with an emphasis on children's literacy. She enjoyed teaching elementary school for well more than a decade and can occasionally be found back in the classroom, talking about books she loves.

Jenny Mollen
Playing Both Sides

It's hard to be anything but agnostic when you grow up with parents who are two different religions. As far back as I can recall, I was presented with two different truths, rendering both somewhat useless.

Maybe if my parents had stayed together longer, they would have picked a specific story and stuck to it, but they divorced when I was two years old, which, upon further review of the VHS home videos, wasn't soon enough.

After their separation, my mother, a hippie shiksa goddess raised Baptist, transformed into a Shirley MacLaine *Pavilion of Past Lives*–type figure. Our house was filled with sage and crystals. She read my aura (I wear the hat of a healer), and she loved sharing stories about how she was my child in our previous lives. I consistently responded, "You're my child in this life!"

While I did attend Catholic school for a year, the only scripture forced down my throat was Richard Bach's *Jonathan Livingston Seagull* and Dan Millman's *Sacred Journey of the Peaceful Warrior*.

When I was seven, we moved to Oregon to be near a dying great-grandmother and my mom's far more religious family. Often left alone, I struggled with anxiety and moral scrupulosity. I remember "testing" God by asking certain questions and then waiting for a variety of religious symbols, such as a burning bush or a new stepdad with money.

It wasn't until I visited my father in Arizona over the summer that I learned about my Ashkenazi Jewish heritage and this other part of my identity. Instead of feeling guilty for not saying my nightly prayers, I felt guilty for ordering a side of bacon with my breakfast.

My problem stemmed from the lack of acceptance I seemed to receive from both families. My mom's family implored me to accept Jesus into my heart, and my father's relatives hated me for never needing to have my nose done.

At a summer camp just outside Bend, someone informed me that my father's Jewish faith would prevent him from entering heaven.

"Jews don't go to heaven because they don't accept Jesus as their savior," she told me.

That was my watershed moment. For me, being Jewish has always felt more like an ethnic identity than a religion. I respect Judaism's teachings and the fundamental concept of deed versus creed, but my deep connection to this group of people who have faced rejection, fear, and oppression throughout history led to my expulsion from the camp for wearing a bikini in the lake and to my bat mitzvah at Jerusalem's Wailing Wall on my fortieth birthday.

I've always needed to fight for the underdog, to champion the outsiders, to be the "other." In some ways, my desire to identify as Jewish was a choice based less on religious preference and more on social justice. People—Jews and gentiles

alike—don't want me to be Jewish. I find it difficult to articulate why this is the case. But it's something I've always
known. It is precisely why I feel so compelled to defy their
wishes and embrace this part of my identity more fully.

As for God, life, and death, I don't know. Do any of us
know? I pray to the universe. And the universe has brought
me to my knees on multiple occasions: when I dropped Sid
on his head and we landed in the E.R., when my father had
a double craniotomy, when my brother ended up in a coma,
and when one of the biggest loves of my life died in my arms.

I hope that there is more after this. As a mother, I would
brave every challenge to reunite with Sid and Lazlo. And I
would ceaselessly search every corner of the afterlife until my
soul could merge with theirs. I might even grab a drink with
Jason if he happens to be in the area.

I believe in past lives, in people who make your heart race
for no apparent reason, in angels, in poodles, in cremation,
in tattoos, and in giant arcs filled with all my ex-boyfriends.
But am I religious? Yes, definitely. And also, no, not at all.

JENNY MOLLEN is a writer, a comedian, and a *New York Times*
bestselling author of the essay collections *I Like You Just the
Way I Am* and *Live Fast Die Hot*, as well as the national bestselling novel *City of Likes*. Heralded by HuffPost as one of the
funniest women on both Twitter and Instagram and named
one of Five to Follow by *T* magazine, Jenny wrote a standing
column for *Parents* magazine and has contributed to *Cosmopolitan, Glamour, New York*, Elle.com, Grubhub, *O, The Oprah
Magazine*, and *Wake Up Call* with Katie Couric. She currently
hosts the show *Dinner and a Movie* on TBS with her husband,
up-and-comer Jason Biggs.

Judy Batalion

Performance Anxiety

"We will attempt to manage the crowd," I was told. "We've had training on how to deflate conflict. Stay silent if in doubt. And, should you need it, we've arranged two forms of emergency egress."

I was not preparing to enter a political debate, but to give a lecture about the Holocaust at an American college campus in 2024. As a professional public speaker, most recently lecturing about my book *The Light of Days*, the story of Jewish women who resisted the Nazis from the ghettos of Poland, I often chat with institutions in advance of my talks. Organizations that hire speakers, for which I am supremely grateful, often have their own social missions, and at times have questions about my material. This is almost never an issue, and these conversations usually serve as fruitful introductions. *Almost* never. I was once invited to do an author interview and a few days before was provided with a detailed script *of my own answers*. Many were wrong! Also, thinking here of a friend's wedding that I emceed, when she gave me the following guidelines: *Under no circumstances can you mention my stepfather, his birth father, or my mother-in-law's estranged second cousin's "alarm" business.* What?!

Sometimes it's me who initiates contact with the organization because I want to know what the audience already knows, especially when I lecture to students. A couple years ago, in the green room at a university hall, it suddenly dawned on me that perhaps these teenagers knew very little about World War II.

"Do these undergrads know what the Holocaust is?" I asked, semi-jokingly, to the event organizer right before he was to introduce me to an enormous lecture room.

He looked at me quizzically, one foot already onstage.

"You know what? I'm not sure. Might be worth explaining it."

Sometimes I speak to organizations first to simply work through practicalities: timing, flow, whether I need a lectern, a slide pointer, or a step (at five-one, I always do). At my own wedding, the caterer had a meltdown during my comedic filibuster, which risked the status of 225 sea bass platings.

But this time, in early 2024, the host organization and I wanted to figure out how to best ensure that the event would be *safe*. This was my first in-person talk since October 7. (Other talks of mine had been postponed or moved to Zoom, where comments were blocked and I was told to run long so there would be no time left for a Q&A.) My presentation would be about the young Jewish women in the underground during the Holocaust: women who ran soup kitchens and orphanages, sabotaged Nazi factories and blew up supply trains, flung Molotov cocktails during ghetto uprisings, and served as couriers, smuggling information, weapons, and hope to Jews locked in ghettos.

My material had nothing at all to do with current events, yet now we were worried: Would the audience's questions be off-topic and inflammatory? Would this event become a protest site, simply because I was "publicly Jewish?" How were we supposed to handle a situation that turned physically threatening? For a few years in my twenties, I performed stand-up comedy in London. Despite several antisemitic heckles that made me feel deeply uncomfortable, and despite my diminutive size, I'd never worried about my physical safety. Now I was facing not only stage fright, but rage fright. I was a mother of three children: Was speaking publicly worth the risk?

Despite years of experience, I still get nervous before a gig. That night, before I went on, my mouth went dry, I was nauseated, and I paced until the auditorium lights dimmed. My body froze, cold, as I ascended the podium and put myself in the spotlight. The firing line.

At the lectern, I grabbed my slide clicker, adjusted my mic, looked out, and took a deep breath. What I saw in front of me, however, was not a band of angry hecklers, but a warm, full house. The region's entire Jewish community, from secular teenagers to the local Chabad rabbis, had come; Jews who had grown up across the United States and the world. As it turned out, this was the first time since October 7 that this school had formally hosted a Jewish-themed event. The moderator introduced me through tears, so moved to finally participate in an event that celebrated the Jewish community. So moved to simply *be together.*

As I talked about the young Jews who fought sickening antisemitism eighty years ago, who fought for our liberty, justice, and dignity, I shook. I understood what it meant to honor the legacy of the women I lectured about, who risked their lives to ensure the continuation of the Jewish people. After all, I realized, none of us at the event were running away from our Judaism. We were all running toward it, toward each other.

JUDY BATALION is the *New York Times* bestselling author of *The Light of Days: The Untold Story of Women Resistance Fighters in Hitler's Ghettos*, which won a National Jewish Book Award and was translated into twenty-four languages, adapted into an award-winning children's book, and optioned by Steven Spielberg's Amblin Partners, for whom Judy cowrote the screenplay. Her first book, *White Walls: A Memoir About Motherhood, Daughterhood, and the Mess in Between*, was optioned by Warner Horizon. Her essays have appeared in the *New York Times*, the *Washington Post*, *Vogue*, and many other publications. Judy is currently writing a novel set in Warsaw in the 1930s.

PART THREE

I Thought We
Were Friends

Jill Zarin

Can You Believe It?

I live in a community in Florida that I like to call "a Jewish ghetto," a saying my mother hates, but it's true. The whole community is Jewish, and I feel very blessed for that. Of course, we were all shocked and horrified to learn about the events of October 7. How could this happen?

I still have trouble wrapping my head around how much hatred and vitriol the attacks unleashed toward our extended community. I have trouble knowing what to do when people online say things that I know are factually untrue. Most people don't *really* know the history of Israel, yet they make claims based on faulty information. How can I just let that happen? How can I watch what happened at the universities this spring and *not* try to get involved?

I decided to use my platform on social media to speak up regularly about antisemitism. I've lost about 30,000 followers as a result, but I'm okay with that. I have to speak up. I repost stories to help educate others and have so much respect for the celebrities, influencers, and notables who have taken their time and energy to do the same. They don't have to do that! But they have shown their support. And it's great. I wish more people would. And, yes, I notice who speaks up and who doesn't. It's hard not to.

In January, I launched a fundraiser for an IDF soldier who performed an incredible mitzvah, surprising a little boy who was a big fan of his and playing guitar for him. It felt so meaningful that I wanted to do something to help. I raised $50,000. Noah came to visit and I was able to raise more money for his troops.

I've noticed that many other Jewish people have now engaged in their Jewishness, not necessarily becoming kosher or going to temple more, but surrounding themselves with Jewish friends. I get that. They want to meet other people who feel the same way they do because they feel abandoned by friends that they thought they had.

I also wanted to find a civil space to engage with friends and strangers who hold different viewpoints. A few months ago, I was having dinner in Palm Beach with two couples, one of whom I'd just met. The woman was sitting across from me, a beautiful woman from Mexico who lives in the States, and we were talking about everything except Israel. But then it came up. She started accusing Israelis, saying specific things that I knew weren't true, but when I tried to point out the inaccuracies, saying, "You don't really believe that, do you?" she got up from the table in the middle of the restaurant and walked out. She grabbed her boyfriend and just said, "We're leaving."

I was haunted by that woman getting up and walking out on me for months. I wanted to say, "Sit back down and let's have a conversation. I want to hear what you have to say. And you should hear what I have to say."

I hope the world finds a solution and that we all find a way to communicate better. I'll keep fighting antisemitism however I can.

JILL ZARIN is a well-known personality, having gained fame as an original cast member of Bravo's *The Real Housewives of New York City*. Prior to that, she had a successful career in the fashion and textile industry. Today, Jill is an entrepreneur, philanthropist, and actress. In 2016, she launched Jill Zarin Home Rugs, alongside Jill Zarin Home Furniture and Jill Zarin Home Tabletop and Accessories. In 2020, Jill and her daughter, Ally Shapiro, launched the wellness and lifestyle brand Jill & Ally. She lives in Florida and the Hamptons. When not working, she enjoys playing tennis and pickleball and spending time with family and friends, including her adorable Pomeranian, Bossi.

Alison Hammer

Scrolling on Shabbat

I t was a Saturday morning this past May or June or July. A Saturday morning "after." I was lying in bed, awake earlier than I needed to be, so I reached for my phone. After playing Wordle (yes, still), I opened Facebook and started to scroll. I scrolled through ads and news alerts and photos of people I might know, until something stopped me. It was a nothing post, the kind of post I'd ordinarily pass right by. But there was something about the nothingness that made me slow down and take a closer look.

The friend who shared it wasn't Jewish, and like so many others, she has been silent about everything happening on the other side of the world. When I looked at her photos from the night before, I didn't just see a barbecue. It wasn't the décor or the meal or the guests that caught my eye. It was a feeling. I saw what appeared to be a carefree life, a glimpse of the way things used to be, the way they were "before."

It struck me, this strange sense of nostalgia for that easy, peaceful way of being. I was jealous that my friend could simply enjoy her weekend. That she could be happy without the shadow of uncertainty and the awareness that there are still more than one hundred men, women, and children being held hostage. That she could walk down the street, sit in the back of an Uber, catch up with an old friend without worrying or even thinking about antisemitism the way I have for the last two, four, six—has it really been eight months?

Then I started to think about what it would take for me to feel that way again. To feel that way now. Today. More than two hundred days since *that* day. I knew that the only way I could move through the world without October 7 weighing heavily on my shoulders, on my mind, and in my heart was if I wasn't a Jew. For a moment, I considered the question: whether I'd be willing to trade my heritage, my history, my religion, and my culture for that feeling of freedom. For the ability to be blissfully unaware of the fire that feels like it's getting closer and closer.

Would I give up the beautiful sound of unified voices chanting and singing in Hebrew during the high holidays? The moment in my favorite prayer where everyone goes from bending down to standing straight and tall? Would I give up lighting the candles on Hanukkah, breaking the fast on Yom Kippur, and making matzo brei on the first weekend morning of Passover?

Would I give up the conventions and community of my high school days in BBYO? Would I give up the sense of connection and belonging I felt the moment I first stepped foot in Eretz Yisrael? Would I give up all the lessons I learned and the lifelong friendships I formed with my Alexander Muss High School in Israel classmates? The moment I picked my

Hebrew name, Mayim, and had it written in tiny letters on a grain of rice in Tel Aviv?

Would I give up those moments of solidarity in the dark, early days when I'd see another member of the tribe? The comfort of sharing a hug and breaking the loud silence as we asked how each other was doing, sharing our worries and our fears? Would I give up the storied history of strength and resilience and badassery of all the generations that came before me?

Would I give *any* of that up to feel free on this Saturday morning in May or June or July? No. Of course I wouldn't.

That certainty and deep knowing felt like a gift, like someone was shining a light on the silver lining that comes with the pain of being targeted. After all, when someone hates you for being who you are, what choice do you have other than to be yourself, but louder and with even more pride?

So I swiped out of Facebook and switched over to Instagram. I kept scrolling, but this time through the curated content of my *chaverim*. My *mishpacha*. And when I saw a post that struck a chord about the hostages or the silence or the blossoming hate, I shared it in hopes of sparking a conversation or a question or a connection with someone else, lying in bed, scrolling on Shabbat.

ALISON HAMMER is half of the writing duo Ali Brady (along with her BFF, Bradeigh Godfrey). Their debut novel, *The Beach Trap*, made several "best of summer" lists, including in the *Washington Post*, the *Wall Street Journal*, *Parade*, and Katie Couric Media. *Until Next Summer*, their third book, is a *USA Today* bestseller. Alison lives in Chicago and works

in Annapolis as an advertising creative director. She is also
the founder and co-president of Artists Against Antisemitism and the author of *You and Me and Us* and *Little Pieces
of Me*. She has no pets, plants, or kids, but she does have
three nephews—two human and one canine.

Toby Rose

On Being the Token Jewish Friend

Years ago, I was introduced to a new friend who was
thrilled to meet someone Jewish.

"Wow," she exclaimed, "I know two other Jewish
people: Jessica Goldberg and Jessica Goldberg's sister!"

Wow, indeed. Though she was from rural Alabama, while
I was from the more cosmopolitan town of Nashville, the feeling was all too familiar. Growing up in Nashville, I was used
to being everyone's token Jewish friend. There is certainly
a thriving Jewish population here; my family was simply not
part of it.

Both of my parents are Jewish, but I was raised in a secular household. My brothers and I were instilled with all the
basic tenets of Judaism without setting foot in a synagogue.
Our parents valued individualism, giving back, and reading. They were small business owners—working hard is part
of my DNA. My mother is an intellectual, and my father is
a master of dirty jokes. We all bonded over movies, never
sports. Oh, and we did love lox and bagels.

Throughout my childhood, I attended schools and lived in parts of town where I became used to being the Other. Living among a community of Christians down here, there were always small offenses but nothing that ever felt anti-semitic. Explaining to friends why I did not have a Christmas tree was a well-practiced habit. Inevitably, there was the all-too-familiar refrain: "But you don't *look* Jewish!"

When I moved away from Nashville after high school, I lived in larger cities where I gravitated toward a more Jewish lifestyle. I lived in Los Angeles for ten years, where I joined Ikar Synagogue, drawn in by the passionate sermons of Rabbi Sharon Brous. I got married under a chuppah to a man who had grown up in a conservative household in Scarsdale, New York.

And when I moved back to Nashville a few years ago, I found that the city had grown exponentially, but some parts remained the same. One of my mother's acquaintances casually described her daughter's new husband: "He's Jewish, but we love him anyway." Last spring, I attended the memorial service for a childhood friend's father. After we hugged, I joked that I had cut the receiving line like I was boarding a Southwest flight.

"That's so Jewish of you," she laughed.

None of these minor offenses ever bothered me—until I had children. We are raising our kids Jewish, and all three attend Hebrew school twice a week. Our sons wear their kippas to class, and I used to worry about them being seen in public. When we stopped for donuts on the way to class, I would think about taking the kippas off their sweet little heads. But the thought hasn't crossed my mind since October 7.

Whereas I used to shy away from being everyone's token Jewish friend, recent events make me want to double down on my Jewish identity. The kids are proud of being Jewish, and so am I. I've loved learning more about Judaism alongside them. We light Shabbat candles on Friday night. I recite the blessings with them and plan to take an adult Hebrew class at Congregation Micah, my current synagogue.

And now I embrace the opportunity to educate my friends. I want to step it up and have the courage to call people out when they make inaccurate comments. I owe this to our children. I owe it to Jessica Goldberg and Jessica Goldberg's sister.

TOBY ROSE is a writer, teacher, and mother living in Nashville, Tennessee. Her work has appeared in *Real Simple*, *Parents*, Kveller, Cup of Jo, and Goop.

Alison Rose Greenberg and Rochelle B. Weinstein

A Bright Light: In Conversation

ROCHELLE: Launch was set for my eighth novel, *What You Do to Me*. October 17, 2023. Finally, the book I'd poured my heart and soul into, the "high-concept" trope for which I'd worked tirelessly to wrangle permissions and artist support, was about to be released. What could go wrong? When I teach publishing workshops at a university in Fort Lauderdale, Florida, I tell my students, "You can do everything right, check every box, and still face unforeseen circumstances." For me, it was October 7. The world stopped. Our collective hearts shattered. The terror and injustice immobilized us. We were glued to our TVs. The last thing on anyone's mind was reading.

ALISON: My sophomore novel, *Maybe Once, Maybe Twice*, published on October 3, 2023. The high, when my novel was chosen as a *Good Morning America* Buzz Pick right before launch, was shortly replaced by a swirl of deep sorrow and guilt. How does one promote a book during a time of unfathomable heartbreak? How does one *not* promote the novel she poured her entire being into? I wasn't sure what the correct answer was to either question.

ROCHELLE: As I grappled with moving forward with my launch event, I received a DM from a Miami pal, Leslie Sharpe: "A friend of mine in Atlanta also has a book coming out this week and this is what some of her friends are posting!"

ALISON: My first book event was an in-conversation scheduled in New York City with Jenny Mollen for October 19. How could Jenny and I talk about sex scenes, second-chance romance, or nineties music at a time like this? How could we dive into the thrills of writing a book during a time of turmoil? Jenny promoted the event on her Instagram, and one of her followers had the same question. She criticized Jenny for promoting *a book* during *a war*. I'll forever be indebted to Jenny for her public response: "If you know anything about what goes into writing a novel you would know that it is a physical and emotional marathon. I'm not going to not support the efforts of another woman and author just because her book is coming out during an apocalypse. I can hold space for both the tragedies of this world and the triumphs of another woman." Jenny's words changed everything. There was a perspective shift that allowed me to embrace my book launch while mourning with my Jewish community. But, even more important, another door opened.

ROCHELLE: I was following the posts. Jenny wrote, "I will still be in conversation with Alison next week because

WOMEN need to always, without question or motive, support other women." I immediately found the author with the book release, Alison Greenberg. I messaged her, and we quickly bonded over the similarities in our stories (music) and how our books were simultaneously entering a traumatized world. Within hours, Alison was welcomed by a team of Jewish authors encircling her and sharing her book.

ALISON: You and Jenny put my book on blast at a time when I felt horrible doing it myself. The instant messages of support that came flying in on Instagram from readers and authors were overwhelming. I went from feeling alone and guilt-ridden to being embraced by the largest virtual hug. Rochelle messaged me, "We are bonded for life now." Watching Rochelle go through her launch so gracefully was an inspiration. I am a screenwriter, and this was only my second novel. My debut novel was published during the pandemic. My second published right before a war, but this time, I didn't feel so alone. I felt a sense of community that an author could only dream of.

ROCHELLE: The world needed joy. And music. And a good read. So our author community did what it always does. They rallied. They lifted. They supported. And that's the essence of all this. The essence of being Jewish. Women. Writers. This is what we do. We may write alone, but we share in each other's triumphs and challenges. Alison and I were in it together, and it didn't stop there. Weeks later, we put together a panel of Jewish authors at the Michael-Ann Russell JCC in Miami to discuss antisemitism and the effects on Jewish authors.

ALISON: I have been involved with the Jewish Book Council, and I was so inspired by everything they were doing to help curb antisemitism in the publishing world. Being up on a panel with Rochelle and other incredible Jewish authors further made me feel like I was no longer on an island by myself.

ROCHELLE: Fast-forward to six months later. I'm in the mountains of North Carolina, and I land on a Facebook post from another Jewish author struggling with her release. I notice she's in conversation with Alison Greenberg in Atlanta, a few hours away. The decision was really simple. My husband and I made plans to drive to Atlanta. We would surprise authors Alison Hammer and Bradeigh Godfrey of Ali Brady books.

ALISON: Looking back on this year, Jenny Mollen's lesson has stayed with me: *We can hold space for tragedies and triumphs.* I will remember the kindness of a stranger, Rochelle—who I now consider family—whose community embraced me as one of their own. I think we can both agree that while the world is forever changed, the unspeakable tragedy of October 7 lives inside of us every day. But finding that small light is what helps us get through.

ROCHELLE: It's no surprise that as we approach the one-year anniversary of the attacks, we're writing this essay in Alison Greenberg's kitchen. It's a new friendship, but it's bound by circumstance and deep trust. Through all the tragedy and suffering of that day, we clung to a single silver lining: what we could do for each other, how we could help. What have we gleaned from October 7? We managed to find the light through the darkness.

ALISON ROSE GREENBERG hails from Atlanta, Georgia, but is quick to say she was born in New York City for the cool factor. Her work has led to multiple pieces of development on both the film and TV side. Among them is an original short story titled *Bad Luck Bridesmaid,* which Alison sold to Working Title as a feature film. She expanded *Bad Luck Bridesmaid* into a novel as part of a two-book deal. Her second novel, *Maybe Once, Maybe Twice,* published in October 2023. She sold her pitch, *Clean Air,* to Amazon Studios. Westbrook, the Chainsmokers, and NASCAR are all producing. Alison speaks fluent rom-com, lives for nineties WB dramas, and cries to indie folk music. She is a proud single mom to two incredible kids, one poorly trained dog, and two cats.

ROCHELLE B. WEINSTEIN is the *USA Today* and Amazon bestselling author of eight novels. She's a book contributor for NBC 6 Miami, *AQUA Magazine,* and Women Writers, Women's Books, splitting her time between the mountains of North Carolina and the beaches of South Florida.

Ali Rosen

We Can Do It with a Broken Heart

My friend's social media post took my breath away. I had to be alone. I excused myself from my kids and family and hid in my parents' garden, tucked away, my headphones in as the bass pumped and the lyrics about crying while being productive landed.

"Do It With a Broken Heart," the song's title instructed.

I'd never really related to Taylor Swift's heartbreak songs, thanks to a less-than-dramatic romantic life. But after being cast aside by my closest friend solely for my Jewishness—and my proximity to a war no one asked for—the music sliced through me. This was a friend so close she came on vacations with my kids and parents across countries and continents. A friend so close she watched my son while my daughters were being born. A friend so close she started a business with my sister.

So how am I in a divorce I never saw coming?

My dad had always warned me to be careful of history repeating itself. He'd said that the antisemitic tropes used for millennia would undoubtedly come back.

"Come on, that couldn't happen in *America*," I'd reply with an eye roll. "We're beyond that."

But then the unthinkable happened in October. In the beginning, I tried to have conversations with anyone who didn't understand the nuance and complexity of the situation. I wanted to showcase our humanity, the way all writers do. After all, our *job* is to slip into someone else's skin. Our job is to see things from all sides, to hurt for all the people who hurt. Most of my non-Jewish friends didn't completely understand, but they were there to listen.

Except for one.

Months later, her flippant social media post brought the pain of betrayal back to the surface again. Sitting in the garden, everything I'd tried to push away rushed back in. My pleas for her to talk rather than avoid. Her antisemitism couched as care. The guy (of course, there's always a guy). The "research" she'd done. The details of our friendship breakup aren't worth revisiting, but the feeling comes uninvited and sits like a puddle that won't evaporate. The idea that someone I knew so intimately could just dismiss me based on my origin is unfathomable, terrifying, and sad.

I thought about a conversation I'd had with my sister a few weeks earlier.

"I feel like my heart is broken," I'd said.

"It is," she'd responded. "And that's okay."

As I sat trying to compose myself while my kids played inside, hiding the grief that months later still could be so easily triggered, I found strength in a pop song about broken hearts. Because unlike the initial hurt of that October day, by now strength had threaded its way through me, a tangible silver lining stitched into the fabric of my heart. Strength came from repeatedly seeing that every single Jewish person

I knew was ready to hold my broken heart. Close friends got closer. Acquaintances I barely knew checked in. Colleagues I'd never spoken to about our mutual Jewishness said, "Let's go out for a coffee." Any Jew I met could see it in my eyes and openly say the things we were all so afraid to say to anyone else, a consistent bulwark in a newly bewildering sea.

The world might be confused about what it means to be Jewish, but we aren't. Sadness and loss have always been a part of being a Jew, and this year has been a stark and scary reminder. But we've always found a way to protect and support each other, even when we disagree (and we often disagree!). We've always survived by our hearts breaking together.

Now I truly understand why Jews call themselves a tribe. We might be disparate, global, of varying political persuasions, belief systems, and even levels of Judaism. But we stand with each other. All the pieces of my broken heart were picked up by every Jewish person who saw me in those months and offered their friendship, leading to the moment in the garden when I knew I would be able to pull myself up again.

This year, I lost my closest friend—but now I know the power of my tribe.

ALI ROSEN is a bestselling author of novels and cookbooks as well as the Emmy- and James Beard Award–nominated host of *Potluck with Ali Rosen* on NYC Life. Her novels—described by *The Skimm* as "a vacation between two covers"—are the instant Amazon bestseller *Recipe for Second Chances* and the Amazon Editors' Pick *Alternate Endings*. Ali is also the author of three cookbooks, including the bestselling *15 Minute Meals*.

She has been featured everywhere from the *Today* show to the *New York Times* and has written for publications including *Bon Appétit*, *Wine Enthusiast*, and *New York* magazine. She is originally from Charleston, South Carolina, but now lives in New York City with her husband, three kids, and rescue dog.

Debbie Reed Fischer

What Stays with Me

I was a sophomore at an international high school in Athens, Greece, when our substitute biology teacher dropped a bombshell: He didn't believe in punishment.

"Do whatever you want. There won't be any consequences, due to my religious beliefs."

I didn't know what this do-whatever-you-want religion was, but amen to that, because I had zero interest in my worksheet on a frog's intestinal tract. After this declaration, the sub sat down and nodded off, signaling our cue to get down to the teen business of slam books, gossip, and flirting. (Ours was not an honors class—think intercontinental version of *Welcome Back, Kotter* with a side of *The Breakfast Club*. Gen X alert!)

The noise level cranked with conversation in multiple languages. A few back-row kids opened a window and lit up cigarettes. Several students walked out.

I started talking to my best friend Tina, a Greek Canadian from Toronto with spiky Duran Duran hair and a brazen confidence I admired. Tina habitually blurted out random questions.

"Why do your mom's friends sound like they're named after Muppets?" she asked on this particular day.

She'd been at my house the prior night and overheard phone calls between my mother and her childhood pals: Etchie, Cuchi, and, my personal favorite, Pupi (pronounced "Poopie"). My mom's friends did, indeed, sound like they lived on Sesame Street.

"It's a Cuban thing," I said and shrugged.

"Wait, you're Cuban?" Stavros piped up. He was the kind of guy who tried to make himself interesting by wearing sunglasses inside. "I thought you were a *JEW*."

He spat-shouted "Jew."

People stopped talking. The only person not focused on this developing story was our substitute, deep in REM-stage sleep.

"Um, I *am*," I answered in a wobbly voice. "Jewish. Cuban. I mean, my mom is from Cuba. And Jewish."

Why did I feel like I was auditioning, as if I needed to prove myself?

"What's wrong with being a Jew?" Tina challenged.

"My father told me Jews are like locusts," Stavros answered casually. "They infest and take over. Never trust a Jew. Parasites."

I was too shocked to speak.

Tina wasn't.

"Your father is disgusting."

People think Canadians are the sweetest people on Planet Earth, and they are, until they have a hockey stick in their hand or someone insults their friends.

"Don't you talk about my father," Stavros warned her from behind his ridiculous sunglasses. "You have no idea who my father is!" Actually, we did. His dad was Someone Important. But most parents at our school were Someone Important, including my father.

I wish I could tell you the whole class dragged Stavros away like in a movie where the bully gets his comeuppance. Nope.

Enter Albert.

Albert was a short, quiet boy from Holland who I was aware of only because of his bowl-cut hairstyle of swingy blond locks that I envied. Also, he wore overalls, unusual attire for a diplomat's kid. He pointed at Stavros.

"Listen, you potato, my grandfather is Jewish."

I don't know if it was little Albert's Dutch accent, his overalls, or the random vegetable insult, but the combo was hilarious.

The class cracked up. It was like a dam broke.

"You and your stupid sunglasses," Albert sneered. "Imbecile, you believe this crap about locusts? Moron." He went on and on, to waves of laughter.

Humiliated, Stavros grabbed his backpack and left.

Why, you may ask, did everyone bust a gut at a dumb potato joke? I have no idea. Yet I went from trembling with fear to shaking with giggles, just moments after hate speech had cut me to my core.

Was it wrong to make fun of someone who'd been taught to dehumanize Jews and didn't know better? Maybe. Should we have woken up the teacher? Maybe, but the man didn't believe in punishment. Should we have attempted a rational convo to counter Stav's hateful comments in a quest to educate him? Maybe. My spidey sense tells me it probably wouldn't have gone too well, though.

So.

I'm grateful for my classmates who took down that bigot with humor, especially Albert. I barely knew him, yet he stood up for me, bravely revealing his family's Jewish background to an antisemite twice his size.

Now more than ever, I remember the courage and humor from that day. Since October 7 and the staggering rise in antisemitism, I feel our collective pain. But I also delight in our ability as a people to find joy in laughter. My Jewish friends and I take action to help, of course. But we also share funny memes, videos, and texts.

Humor turns insults into punch lines and adversity into strength. It helps take fear away. If we can laugh, hate won't win.

When one of my first young-adult novels launched, *Kirkus Reviews* stated: "Fischer balances weighty issues with a sharp wit." My editor said it was the humor that convinced him to acquire my book, despite the disturbing subject of bullying. I'm currently writing a novel based on my family in Cuba on the eve of World War II, when my uncle was a passenger on the infamous Voyage of the Damned, the *St. Louis*. I find myself writing humorous scenes as well as sad ones.

Humor saved me that day in tenth grade, and it saves me today.

Perhaps I have Tina, Albert, and even that potato Stavros to thank for that.

Would you like to know what happened to them?

I fell in love with wee Albert. Too bad our romance lasted only twenty-four hours. Albert moved to Japan the next day. That's an international school for you.

Tina lives in Greece and teaches at a private school.

Stavros follows me on Instagram. Now he goes by Steve, is sans sunglasses in his profile pic, and "likes" my posts with Jewish content. "Steve" seems different from Stavros. Does he remember what he said to me? Has he changed?

I don't know, but I've changed. I'm done auditioning.

What stays with me is the strength of humor and the glimmer of hope when allies surface in unexpected places. In the face of hate, laughter prevailed.

How Jewish.

DEBBIE REED FISCHER is an award-winning author of novels for teens and tweens. Her middle-grade novel *This Is Not the Abby Show* won the Royal Palm Literary Gold Award for Best Children's Book and was twice honored as a PJ Library selection, in 2017 and 2020. Debbie has been teaching writing workshops as well as speaking on author panels, at schools, and at literary conferences for many years. In addition to writing novels, Debbie has contributed to TV and film scripts, anthologies, nonfiction books, magazines, and newspapers. A graduate of the University of Miami, Debbie has a degree in Screenwriting and worked for many years as an agent for film and TV, then as a teacher, before achieving her dream of becoming an author. Her forthcoming book is a historical novel, set in 1939 Guantánamo, Cuba, based on her family on the eve of World War II.

PART FOUR

An (Unlikely?) Activist

Samantha Ettus

Double Date

October 7, 2023, had been marked on my calendar for years. I knew the day would be an important one: the day of my son's bar mitzvah. As we danced and celebrated with family and friends, we heard rumblings of trouble in Israel, but had no sense of the gravity of what had happened. Even the cantor naïvely ran off to officiate his niece's wedding.

The next morning, I'd planned to scour through photos to make a bar mitzvah highlight reel. But when I woke up, read and saw what had happened in Israel, I quickly forgot the hora; I needed to learn about the horrors. The laughter, themed food stations, and photo booth were replaced by details of the massacre, which I felt compelled to post. I found myself sifting through unthinkable stories and horrific images and a lot of misinformation. I was on a desperate hunt for the truth.

I posted about the atrocities for a few days, assuming I'd return to my regularly scheduled programming when the "grown-ups" arrived, like the Middle East experts and Jewish intellectuals. But they never showed up. They were probably too busy advising or strategizing about how to respond to the attacks to post themselves.

Within days people started looking to me for news. Me! It felt like when someone is waving at you, but you know that can't be the case, so you turn to see if there's someone behind you instead. And yet, I quickly found my place as someone who could distill information and make it digestible against a misleading sea of propaganda.

The cast of characters who joined me every day on social media to fight for Israel and against antisemitism felt like a ragtag crew: we were a former marketer, a small business owner, an author, a dietician, a reality star, an actor, and more. At the time I couldn't have imagined that this group of "Jewish influencers" would be the people who I'm now honored to refer to as "my colleagues." We aren't the IDF or the academics or the sages; we are a new kind of Jewish warrior, inscribing our part in the 3,500-year history of our people through each post.

As a Hebrew School dropout, I originally felt intensely unequipped to play the role I found myself inhabiting. There was absolutely no room for error, so I had to get educated— and fast. I read voraciously beginning with Noa Tishby's *Israel*, moving on to Dara Horn's *People Love Dead Jews*, and then on to *Exodus*, a novel I'd never read and always meant to. These books and a slew of podcasts began to fill some of the deep gaps in my understanding of Middle East history and Israeli culture.

My late mother (yeshiva-educated, yet resentful about it) would be stunned to see me today. Her rabbi father, even more so. I have fallen in love with the history and the land and the people. I am more Jewish than ever before, not in religion but in attachment. The unsettling silence of my former friends feels less deafening than it first did; the air is now filled with the voices of all my new friends and colleagues. The "tribe" that I had always heard about was real, and it was astoundingly comforting.

My son is a thoughtful old soul. He was troubled by forever sharing his bar mitzvah date with the date of the atrocities. I told him that this is the bittersweet beauty of life. Pain and celebration often coexist. On that horrifically historic day, something beautiful happened, too.

SAMANTHA ETTUS is a national bestselling author of five books, a renowned speaker, and a former co-host of iHeart's leading women in business podcast. Sam was a longtime contributor to *Forbes* and was a syndicated columnist for Scripps Howard News Service. For many years, Sam hosted a national call-in radio show and was host of leading internet talk show "Obsessed TV," which she created and produced with internet personality Gary Vaynerchuk.

Sam has spoken on hundreds of stages across America from TEDx to Fortune 500 companies and Jewish Federations. She has appeared on many TV shows and has been featured in every major print outlet. Sam earned both her undergraduate and MBA degrees from Harvard. She is a proud mom of three teenagers.

Aliza Licht

Being a Jewish Activist Wasn't on Brand for Me

"What's on brand for you?"

That is the question I posed to every potential reader of my book, *On Brand*, when it debuted in April 2023. I had total clarity on my personal brand. It fell neatly into a Venn diagram with facets of fashion, marketing, social media, career advice, and personal branding strategy. However, one of the foundational exercises of establishing a personal brand is first identifying your belief system and your brand guardrails. Where do you have permission to play versus when you should opt out? I knew those answers like the back of my hand, so much so that I could teach others. So much so that I had a book published about my personal branding expertise.

My brand guardrails were very clear until October 7, 2023. On that day, I needed to penetrate the well-defined exterior of my personal brand and probe into who I was at the core. Deep inside, my belief system was loud and clear: I am a proud Jew, the granddaughter of not one but *four* Holocaust survivors initially born in Poland and Austria. Sure, I had spoken up against antisemitism here and there before (I'm looking at you, Kanye), but those were light raindrops of advocacy nowhere near the ocean waves of activism a few of my peers displayed. Me an activist? Never. But then it all changed.

A few weeks before October 7, the Instagram account @endjewhatred randomly messaged me via DM, asking if I would be willing to collaborate on an Instagram post sharing my view on why it's essential to speak up against antisemitism. When I read the DM, my initial reaction was: *Sure, but not now.* Not now, because my gut told me it needed to be tied to something happening and relevant; otherwise, it would stick out on my Instagram feed like a sore thumb. Why draw attention to antisemitism during a time of relative quiet? In truth, I was slightly disappointed in myself for even thinking that. Fighting against antisemitism shouldn't be convenient or timely; it's too important. But my brand guardrails popped into my head, and while being proudly Jewish is always who I am, speaking on this subject did not fit nicely into my social media content buckets.

On October 7, I was in Las Vegas for a fun, carefree weekend. When I learned about the horrific Hamas crimes against humanity in Israel, I was stunned in horror. While checking Instagram DMs, there was @endjewhatred again asking if I would make a video about the terror attack. Standing in the loud and buzzing lobby of the Wynn hotel, I could not wrap my head around being able to do this. But then my brain kicked into gear, and I realized that not only could I do this, but it was also my duty. My grandparents did not survive the horrors of the Holocaust for me to be silent.

I posted my first video. Once it went live, something changed in me. The obligation I felt was palpable, but more than that, it became evident that I was speaking for every Jewish person in my network, many of whom at the time had not even fathomed that they would be advocating for Israel publicly. You see, this advocacy was always in the shadows in Jewish circles. IYKYK. We knew better than to flaunt our Jewishness. Staying under the radar was safer and more comfortable.

That video led to the next and the next on Instagram, combined with curating reliable news sources worldwide.

This pivot shocked some of my most loyal and long-standing followers and readers of my books. One follower reached out on X to express his disappointment. His tweet stopped me dead in my tracks. His earnest message reminded me that I needed to explain, to give context, and to make him, hopefully, and many others understand. My response was lengthy and thoughtful. It felt good to respond in what I hoped was a productive manner. I pinned the tweet to my profile to ensure others could see it.

Since then, I have used my personal brand to stand with Israel and to lend my voice to others. My mission is to give people who trust me my advice and to share my worldview to give others strength and the historical knowledge they need. I've done it to show my community that they can be brave and stand up.

As a brand consultant and social media strategist, creating content is part of what I do. That's the easy part. Watching the hatred and ignorant responses pile up in my feed was hard initially, but when you believe something so authentically, and you come from a place of knowledge, that gives you strength.

I am now fearless, and nothing makes me happier than seeing people in my network who have leveraged their personal brands on social media to stand with Israel, too.

We all wake up each day scared to see what horrors happened while we were sleeping. Who hates us now? We live in a constant state of rage about the lies and propaganda being spread to discredit and blame Israel and the Jews.

My grandmother Hilda, who survived the concentration camps, taught me to believe people when they show you who they are for the first time. Hamas's mission is clear; wiping Israel off the earth and killing Jews around the world is quite literally in their charter. They have publicly vowed to repeat October 7 "over and over again." The Western world needs to stand up against terrorism, because what starts with Jews doesn't end with Jews. We are just an easy target.

On October 7, I stopped sharing *other* social media content for six months. I paused promoting my book, publishing new episodes of my podcast, and recording future episodes. I became a trusted news source and voice on Instagram for many Jews around the world living in this very real nightmare. I still am. People warned me that I would lose followers by doing so. I've more than doubled my following. The Jews are fighting. We will not be silent. Never again is *now*.

Becoming an activist was not on my bingo card. It was never part of my personal brand. But I was wrong. Standing with Israel and fighting antisemitism has never felt more on brand for me.

ALIZA LICHT is an award-winning marketer, a bestselling author, a podcaster, a personal branding expert, and a career development coach. With more than twenty-five years in the fashion and media industries, she has extensive experience in branding and online storytelling. As the founder of Leave Your Mark, a multimedia brand and consultancy, she advises businesses and individuals on brand strategy. A social media pioneer and one of the first fashion influencers, Aliza was the anonymous force behind the DKNY PR GIRL phenomenon.

Her first book, *Leave Your Mark: Land Your Dream Job. Kill It in Your Career. Rock Social Media.* (2015), offers career mentorship and advice for early professionals. Her podcast of the same name has more than 1.5 million downloads and is produced by Money News Network. Named one of "America's Next Top Mentors" by the *New York Times* and one of *Business Insider*'s "Top 20 Most Innovative Career Coaches," Aliza is a recognized global mentor.

Her second book, *On Brand: Shape Your Narrative. Share Your Vision. Shift Their Perception.* (2023), is a comprehensive guide to personal branding and won the Best Book of 2023 in Business: Marketing and Advertising by American Book Fest. Regularly featured in the media, Aliza has appeared on *Good Morning America*, the *Today* show, E!, Bloomberg, and more.

Lisa Barr

Loud and Proud: The Voice in My Head

An elderly woman with sass in her step approached me after my book gig in Greenville, South Carolina. It was early June, my first out-of-town event for my new novel, and, admittedly, I was exhausted and raw from the onslaught of relentless antisemitism—particularly in the book world.

Since October 7, I, along with many Jewish authors and artists, have experienced a tsunami of harassment (at least fifty times a day I receive some form of a "Die Jew" message), review-bombing (more than 450 one-star reviews beginning on October 8 in a coordinated attempt to tank my work), and dealing with book event cancellations—for one reason only: I am a loud and proud Jewish author who refuses to remain silent.

I'm also the triple threat—the daughter of a Holocaust survivor, a former journalist who worked for the *Jerusalem Post* and lived in Israel for seven years, and an author of World War II thrillers. In other words: prime time for the haters.

Ironically, as a young journalist, I covered one of the most important historical moments of almost peace between enemies: the Oslo Accords—the famous "handshake" between the late (assassinated) prime minister of Israel Yitzhak Rabin, the late PLO leader Yasser Arafat, and President Bill Clinton at the White House.

Ahh, if only . . .

The woman leaned over the table as I signed two books that she bought for her daughters-in-law and said: "I'm not sure how to say this. I know it's gonna come out all wrong, but, hell, I'm gonna say it anyway: The Jews just never give up—and I love that . . . just love it. Shame on those haters. You . . ."

She pointed between my eyes, "Keep fighting back—just like your main character in your book. She doesn't stop, and don't you stop, either." There, right there.

I froze with my black Sharpie in midair. The woman's words echoed in the room—treasured words that belonged to my beloved grandmother. It was as if my Grandma Rachel had materialized from Heaven's Kitchen (where she serves as executive chef) and put her own voice into this woman's mouth to remind me during this difficult time to stay strong, stay in my lane, and remember what she'd taught me way back when I was just a girl in her kitchen.

My grandmother, a Holocaust survivor, was my best friend, my personal heroine, and will always be the voice in my head. Her parents and siblings perished in Auschwitz, but her immediate young family survived the war. She exemplified the beauty of family, the power of tradition, and taught me to fight for those you love no matter what. She encouraged me to use my voice (and words) to stand up to hate, even if I'm scared—especially if I'm scared.

LISA BARR

And I've been plenty scared and worried these days by the rampant antisemitism worldwide, the virulent hatred toward Jews and Israel on college campuses, and the vandalizing of Jewish businesses à la Kristallnacht, and perhaps most disturbing is that antisemitism has become trendy among the younger set. As someone who has covered terrorism extensively, I wish I could stand on a mountaintop and shout: *Terrorism knows no boundaries. Be careful what you wish for, kids . . .*

How I wish my grandmother were by my side right now in real time. If only I could feel the wrinkled softness of her hand encasing mine as I navigate this new normal. She would see a different me, emerging post–October 7—a woman who wears her Judaism every day, not just on Shabbat when I light the candles.

My daily jewelry is now super-Jewy—a chai and a Jewish star necklace, a Jewish star bracelet, a dog tag for the hostages, and a gold ring with my Hebrew name on it that I bought with my babysitting money when I was sixteen and on my teen tour to Israel. It's my armor and message to the world: I will never cower.

Perhaps antisemitism is no different than it's ever been. Maybe things never really changed post-Holocaust. The difference now is that many of us are not afraid to stand up, band together, use our resources, and fight back.

Now, nearly a year after the massacre in Israel and all that has ensued, the blacklists and harassers don't scare me the way they did in the beginning. Recently, I even told one antisemitic woman at one of my book events who tried to tear me down mid-presentation that we should "have coffee." Her blatant goal was to see me shrink, but instead, I used the opportunity to stand taller, to take the higher road, and to show all those around us the ugly face of hate: hers. She later apologized and wrote to me privately, "I have much to learn."

The legacy of October 7 has been an unfathomable, unending nightmare, but also a calling and an awakening for Jews worldwide. I am forever changed as an author, a journalist, a mother of three daughters, a human.

On October 6, I knew what I wanted from life, but after October 7, I knew what life wanted from me: putting my grandmother's voice and her legacy of survival into real action.

"Loud and proud" is the new "Never again."

LISA BARR is the *New York Times* and *USA Today* bestselling author of *The Goddess of Warsaw*, *Woman on Fire*, *The Unbreakables*, and the award-winning *Fugitive Colors*. Lisa served as an editor for the *Jerusalem Post*, managing editor of *Today's Chicago Woman*, managing editor of *Moment* magazine, and as an editor/reporter for the *Chicago Sun-Times*. Among the highlights of her career, Lisa covered the famous "handshake" between the late Israeli Prime Minister Yitzhak Rabin, the late PLO leader Yasser Arafat, and President Bill Clinton at the White House. Lisa has been featured on *Good Morning America* and the *Today* show for her work as an author and journalist. Actress Sharon Stone has optioned the rights to adapt *Woman on Fire* for film.

Stacy Igel

Stand Up!

I remember the call and the questioning—whether I wanted to be part of a commercial produced by Robert Kraft standing up to Jewish hate, a decision that would mean giving up perpetual rights to my own image. Should I do it? I thought back to the time when I wasn't allowed to participate in ballroom dancing with my friends at their club because I was Jewish. My father called the club and firmly declared, "You *will* allow my daughter in with her friends." He stood up for me and got me in. How could I not stand up for this commercial?

I said yes.

The commercial aired close to the publication date of my first book, *Embracing the Calm in the Chaos*, in March 2023, well before October 7, and featured my face as the center image of people standing up to Jewish hate. When I tell you my inbox, DMs, texts, and calls were flooded with thank-yous, it's an understatement. Many in my professional life after college may not have known I was Jewish. I was not one to broadcast my Jewish identity everywhere—not because I wasn't proud, but because I never felt the need to. Suddenly, everyone knew. Friends I hadn't heard from in fifteen years, who still had my first cell phone number from back in the day, texted me.

"I just saw your face and statement during the Giants game. Thank you," they said.

I was mad at myself for even questioning being involved in the ad.

My late grandfather, "Pap Doc," started a tradition where all my family members—cousins, aunts, uncles, sisters, parents, and friends—would meet in a central place for the Passover holiday, no matter where we all were in the world. Pap Doc passed away in 1980, but after his passing, my Nana Rose continued the tradition, and after her passing my mom, aunt, uncle, and my sister and cousins have upheld it ever since.

I vividly remember one Passover when my cousin's dear friend Rachel, now the mother of Hersh Goldberg-Polin, taught us a cup game. We would pass the cups we were holding to the person next to us, all to a song that still plays in my head. When the song ended, if you were out of a cup, you were out of the game.

When the attacks on October 7 happened, I learned that Rachel's son, Hersh, had been taken hostage. My heart plummeted. Since then, all I have done is pray and help raise awareness to bring Hersh and the other hostages home. Suddenly the commercial that was released in March 2023 came back on the air. My face fighting antisemitism became a symbol in people's homes at a time when we all needed it the most.

This year, as we sat around the Passover table with so many family members and friends, we set an empty seat and left a chair open for the hostages, praying for them, along with all the innocent lives affected by the war. As my grandfather predicted years ago, "In the years to come, there will be many changes in the world, in the country, and most of all in us."

Over the past year, antisemitism around the world has escalated dramatically. I have personally witnessed more incidents, and my colleagues have, too—musicians, artists, authors, designers, and more. As someone who has dedicated their life to bringing people together and creating a brand that does the same, I urge readers to understand the pain so many of us are experiencing worldwide and to join us in the fight against antisemitism. Use your voice to stand up. We must come together to stop hate.

STACY IGEL is the founder and creative director of BOY MEETS GIRL®, a global impact brand known for its iconic double-silhouette logo and purposeful, edgy, contemporary athleisure wear. Stacy has had exclusive fashion partnerships with Paris's Colette, Bergdorf Goodman, Saks Fifth Avenue, and Target, among others. She collaborates with musical artists, athletes, and activists making an impact, as well as organizations including the Young Survival Coalition, BullyBust, Human Rights Watch, Youth Over Guns, and more. Stacy and BOY MEETS GIRL® have been featured in *Elle, Cosmopolitan, Teen Vogue, Women's Wear Daily,* the *New York Times,* and dozens more. She is the cocreator/cohost of the podcast #MOMSGOTTHIS, featured in *Forbes* as a "women-created podcast everyone should be listening to right now." Stacy is a frequent lecturer and panelist on subjects like social media, philanthropy, branding, and entrepreneurship. Her first book, *Embracing the Calm in the Chaos: How to Find Success in Business and Life Through Perseverance, Connection, and Collaboration*, covers her entrepreneurial journey and provides practical tips and takeaways for others to use in life and in business.

Elizabeth Cohen Hausman

Using My Voice

I was born and raised on the Upper East Side of Manhattan, where I grew up a Reform Jew. I attended Hebrew school, was bat mitzvahed, and celebrated the high holidays, and that was about it. While I wasn't deeply religious, Judaism brought joy to my home, where my parents embraced Jewish culture.

My parents married young and experienced a lot of sadness; their parents all died young. While love was a constant in our home, I always felt an undercurrent of insecurity, like everything was tenuous and fragile. My mom and dad always said they were "just happy my sister and I were alive and healthy," but it wasn't that simple to me. I felt like everything could easily be lost: our possessions, our apartment.

My parents were kind and empathetic, extending a warm welcome to friends and fostering children from Africa. Their empathy left an indelible mark on my life; there was no person or animal who wouldn't get the warmest embrace from my entire family.

In high school, I unknowingly suffered from attention deficit disorder (ADD), which wreaked havoc on my teenage years. I was manic. My mind was unfocused. I ran from place to place and friend to friend. I lashed out. I struggled mightily in school. I wanted to run and didn't know why, but had no place to run *to*. I found solace in the homes of my classmates. Every chance I got, I set out to explore New York City. The world of the 1980s was exciting: clubs, parties, glamor, and bright lights. I craved them all.

And yet it was during those wild years that I developed an acute appreciation for the Holocaust. It fascinated me. It traumatized me. I read countless books, went to museums, and watched many movies on the subject. I listened to the stories of those lost. While school bored me and I didn't pay much attention in history class, the Holocaust and its sheer brutality and unfairness kept me captivated. Back then, I had no idea *how* Hitler rose to power in the 1930s, nor did I analyze *why* America stayed out of the war until Pearl Harbor, but what sunk in was that 6 million innocent people had been systematically exterminated.

My people.

How could that have happened? What kind of person could perpetrate such horrific crimes? What if it happened again? Would anyone protect my family and me? Could it happen in New York? Could we be taken from our home and murdered like them, simply because we were Jewish?

As I learned about the Holocaust and the senseless tragedy perpetrated on such a grand scale, my appreciation of my religious and cultural affiliation escalated. *Those people were killed because they were Jewish. And, yes, the Nazi murders were indiscriminate. But I'm Jewish. I would be dead, or, if I lived, my*

friends and family would likely be dead. Would anyone protect me?
What if I had been Anne Frank?

Obviously, the Holocaust is a dark subject. And like all terrible times, no one wants to think about it, let alone relive it. But Jews are always reminded to "never forget." Could there be any wiser words? *What* and *who*, exactly, shouldn't be forgotten? To me, the answer is hate. Every Jewish person must remember that hateful people can be cruel on unspeakable levels.

So what does being Jewish mean to me now?

First, being Jewish is a kinship with all of those lost souls and families devastated by the Holocaust, families sent to their deaths in the most horrific and evil ways. Gas chambers, starvation, unbelievable cruelty.

Second, being Jewish is my voice. I want everyone to know that I am here and present and that no Holocaust is going to silence me as a Jew, a mother, and everything else that I am.

Third, being Jewish is a message. I will remind everyone I can that we can never forget. As it is said, history is doomed to repeat itself.

Finally, being Jewish is hope. While it's insane to even think about who would hide me, I know that I would hide others, and I very much hope they would do the same for me.

Today, I am a woman in my fifties. I have kids and a Jewish husband. I have seen life, death and illness, happiness and sadness of all kinds. My children have a stronger Jewish identity at this point in their lives than I did at their age, but they still don't really understand the Holocaust. I worry that they won't passionately understand and teach its lessons.

The recent events of October 7, 2023, have further shaped my Jewish identity. I was startled, furious, and devastated that attacks on the innocent could happen today simply because the victims were Jewish. The news tapped into all of the devastation I felt about the Holocaust. The destruction of the innocent. The violence. Senseless rage against Jews.

How people have reacted to the attacks has, and continues to, upset me. I take the opportunity to speak out against antisemitism, the targeting of Jews for no other reason than their identity. Hate contradicts the very foundations of empathy and kindness my parents taught my sister and me. While some friends may say they understand my pain, I'm not sure that the acts of barbarism or even my struggles with the attacks are actually important to them. It all consumes me.

Recently, in an effort to build awareness, I hosted a big screening in Southampton of the Sheryl Sandberg documentary "From Screams to Silence." That evening, I brought over the sisters of a hostage from Israel to share their pain and struggle. Amazingly, their message of hope shined through. The situation is heartbreaking and complicated. I pray that the war ends soon, the hostages return safely, and a peace can be found for all involved.

Being Jewish means that I am a proud part of a community that will forever need a voice against hate. And I am using mine.

ELIZABETH COHEN HAUSMAN is a native New Yorker who is a seasoned public relations professional and strategist spanning three decades. She is a tastemaker primarily focused on fashion, events, and brand marketing. She is devoted to philanthropy. Elizabeth is a cochair with her husband, James Hausman, of ADAPT Leadership Awards Gala, a New York–based charity serving the developmentally disabled with nearly four thousand employees. She is an avid supporter of causes focused on animal rescue and regularly works with support animals. She is also an ardent advocate against antisemitism. Elizabeth lives in New York with her husband and two children.

Rebecca Minkoff

Be the Change

I remember very clearly waking up on October 7 and heading downstairs to grab my instant caffeine fix. But what happened instead is that my dear friend began to relay to me the horrors that had unfolded as we slept. She was visibly shaken, unsure if her relatives and family had been attacked and killed. I spent what should have been a relaxing weekend in the woods attached to my phone, taking in image after image of the unspeakable: innocent women and children murdered, tortured, raped.

What seemed like something out of a nightmare unfolded into our reality. Initially, I was viewing the horrific acts of terrorism and violence from a distance. It was "over there," and I felt that I was safe in America, a country where nothing like this could ever take place. And then the unthinkable happened, something my mom had been saying for years was being stirred up on our soil. A sentiment I thought was her being neurotic and pessimistic.

Antisemitism.

In America, and really everywhere I have traveled, I never once felt unsafe or at risk as a Jewish woman. That has changed dramatically since October 7.

Day after day, I am seeing the rising rates of people coming forward unabashedly flaunting their hatred of Jews, while others offer complicit silence and stay out of it, claiming the issues are too complicated.

I named my newsletter "You Can't Make This Up," because as a woman in business, it's always shocking to hear how other founders have pulled off miracles and grown in spite of them. But what you really can't make up right now is the license to hate, the license to align with terrorism, and the silence of so many leaders and allies alike not taking a stand.

We are at a time in history that allows news to spread fast and for everyone to have a voice, but the voices we need speaking up right now are ones that stand up to antisemitism, actively fight hate, and dare to challenge breeding grounds and education systems that have been put in place to perpetuate this upon future generations.

If you are in a position of power in the business world, I implore you to do the following:

1. Form teams at work with people who don't espouse racist or anti-religious views.
2. Speak out if you see antisemitism in the workplace.
3. Reassess your involvement with institutions that promote violence against Jews or any other race or religion.

There are 16 million of us. We have been fighting off attacks for generations. In the internet age, one that we thought would push humanity forward, it appears technology is only hastening barbarism, atrocities, and unbearable violence.

We have the power to alter the outcome of this era.

Be the change. Have the courage. Speak out.

REBECCA MINKOFF is an industry leader in accessible luxury handbags, accessories, and apparel, whose playful and subtly edgy designs integrate the elements of bohemian femininity with a little bit of rock 'n' roll. After developing an affinity for design while in the costume department in high school, Rebecca moved to New York City at eighteen to pursue her dream of becoming a fashion designer. In 2001, Rebecca designed a version of the "I Love New York" T-shirt as part of a five-piece capsule collection. In 2005, Rebecca designed her first handbag, which she soon dubbed the "Morning After Bag," aka the M.A.B. This iconic bag ignited Rebecca's career as a handbag designer and inspired her feminine creations in the years to come. After four years of designing statement-making handbags and accessories with her trademark leathers, studs, and hardware, Rebecca introduced her first ready-to-wear collection in 2009. Today, Rebecca Minkoff is a global brand with a wide range of apparel, handbags, footwear, jewelry, and accessories. In September 2018 she established the Female Founder Collective, a network of businesses led by women that invests in women's financial power across the socioeconomic spectrum by enabling and empowering female-owned businesses.

Alyssa Rosenheck

Rest and Responsibility

"In six days, G-d created the heavens and the earth—and on Shabbat, He rested."

And so did we (ish).

I recently found myself in the holiest of cities, on the holiest of days: Jerusalem, observing Shabbat with friends. As the sun began to set, the weathered and worn stone of the city reflected the warmth of its descent. The divinity of Jerusalem's history became apparent in the stillness of the streets and the sounds of prayer filling the air.

Jerusalem is a city of profound dichotomies, much like the times we live in now. Though small and narrow in geography, its depth holds a history rich with both pain and hope. It is a city that has faced destruction and resurrection. It honors its ancient traditions while welcoming in the technology of the new—Israel is called the "Startup Nation" for good reason.

I have grown comfortable with the dichotomies here because don't we all carry them within ourselves? Themes of death and rebirth, war and peace, control and surrender, goodbyes and faith-filled new beginnings. Even as I made my way to the home of our hosts via Route 443, picking up delicate, soft flowers as a hostess gift, I was cognizant of the extremes.

I seek peace, but I, too, have a war within. I desire freedom, yet fight the oppression of my own fears. I seek alignment in the present, shedding limiting narratives from my past. I strive for justice while I long for mercy. I aim to reconcile who I was on October 6 with who I am now in a post–October 7 world, where each day still feels like the 8th.

I've been to Israel twice since the war began. Initially, I traveled to a war zone to make sense of the conflict in the States. What I found was not what I expected; I found love and home. This land represents more than just a conflict. It embodies resilience and a profound sense of belonging.

I walked into my friend Fleur Hassan-Nahoum's home in historic Jerusalem and was greeted with warmth. The lights were low, her kaftan shimmered, and the glow of candlelight illuminated the four walls of her family's house. The antique table was set for fifteen people, graced with traditional Jewish, Moroccan, and Iraqi recipes that have endured exile and centuries of tradition. The heartfelt, deep conversations around her table anchored the space. I was in town as a delegate, spending most of my time in the south near the Gaza border and in meetings in Tel Aviv, while others in the room had come from all over the world, either as friends or for an AI conference centered on creativity.

As I soaked up the conversations, new names, and fascinating stories, all of a sudden, I heard the word "Jew" in a conversation behind me. It jolted me physically; my jaw tensed. I was reminded of the death threats, the war, the hostages, the lost book deal for being Jewish, and the derogatory remarks about my identity that I've faced in the States. It brought me back to the reality of why I was there, a reminder of the complexities and tensions underpinning the physical war we are winning just miles away and the ideological battles I fight on the digital frontlines back in America.

In a room filled with a rich tapestry of ideas, backgrounds, and peace, the single word "Jew" reverberated with the weight of the world.

In that moment, I felt the profound connection between the ancient and the modern, the personal and the political, the love and the loss. My heartbeat quickened, a quiet roar signaling the pride I have in our shared history and the traditions we uphold every Friday night. The warmth of Fleur's home, the spirited dialogue, and the breaking of bread were more than hospitality; they embodied acts of fortitude, defiance against the odds, and unity in a time when all of us are facing our own battles.

Israel is our mirror.

In this land of dichotomies, I've gained a deeper understanding: Life's light, like the candles lit in prayer, balances rest and responsibility. This deep sense of belonging brings with it an obligation: to uphold our shared values, fight for our peace and for our homeland, and confront the challenges before us with courage. It is in this balance of rest and responsibility that we find our true strength and purpose.

On Shabbat, we still. We ground ourselves in community, we love, and we renew. In the morning, we rise again to create and face the challenges that await. While my body may be conditioned to react with alertness upon hearing the word "Jew" in 2024, my heart will always respond with love. For in my Jewishness, I am forever home.

ALYSSA ROSENHECK is a celebrated interiors and architectural photographer, a bestselling author, a speaker, and an advocate. Recognized by *Architectural Digest* and featured in more than nine hundred magazines, Alyssa is renowned for her work capturing the essence of homes across the United States. Alyssa authored the bestselling book *The New Southern Style* and is a sought-after speaker on "creative courage." Her work and insights have been featured in prominent publications like *Forbes, People, Vogue,* and *Good Grit* magazine.

Beyond her creative achievements, Alyssa is a dedicated Pro-Israel advocate and a founding member of Artists Against Antisemitism. With a decade of experience capturing homes across the U.S., she passionately advocates for our collective home through her education on antisemitism and her experiences as a delegate in Israel. Her journey of resilience, marked by overcoming cancer, and her commitment to service inspire and unite aspiring entrepreneurs, creatives, and advocates alike.

Rachel Barenbaum

What Can Happen to a Woman in Nine Months?

After Shabbat services, we filed out to the social hall and gathered for kiddush, to bless the wine and challah before eating lunch. It was a hot day, and the air-conditioning wasn't working. I felt sweat on the backs of my knees and hoped I didn't have a mark on my dress where it folded at my stomach while I sat. It was a silly thing to worry about, to think anyone would notice, because this Shabbat was the one that marked nine months since October 7, 2023.

Nine months. The timing made me sick to my stomach. I knew I wasn't the only one, because almost every woman I'd spoken to that morning had already mentioned it. Every week during services we read the names of every hostage out loud. This week as we read them, one person added the question *What can happen to a woman in nine months?*

In the social hall, we said kiddush and motzi and I went through the buffet line for a bagel. This week the synagogue had ordered whitefish salad. It's usually my favorite Shabbat treat, but I wasn't sure I could eat anything. I took only a little.

I sat down with two girlfriends, women I sit with almost every week after services. We have children the same age and usually talk about how we're trying—and failing—to balance career and kids, or politics and books. We chat about things that matter and things that don't. But we're quiet.

"The women?" I ask.

They understand my question, that I'm asking if we're all thinking about the women and the nine-month marker. Nine months is loaded with meaning for every woman. We'd started talking about it four weeks earlier because at least one of us had given birth at eight months. We'd seen this coming.

"What can happen to a woman in nine months?" I asked. "Have you seen the campaign on social media?"

They all nodded.

"I don't know if I can talk about it," one said.

I'd known this friend long enough to know why she didn't want to talk about it, but I couldn't let it go.

"If we don't talk about it, who will?" I asked.

What can happen to a woman in nine months? Rape. Birth.

I couldn't stop thinking about it. I looked at my friends. We'd all lived the cycle, all had children.

"There could be more Jewish hostages now than there were nine months ago," I said.

According to Jewish law, if your mother is Jewish, you are Jewish.

"It makes me sick that the world denies it," one friend said. I felt the same way.

"#BelieveWomen apparently only applies to non-Jewish women," my other friend said.

Rape. The hostages were raped. There was no question about it. I'd watched the images of Israeli women being taken on October 7. I saw blood on their pants, the way it stained the fabric between their legs. And I cried. I still cry when I think about it. Blood doesn't just appear between a woman's legs, not like that.

I knew it the minute I saw those photos. My children looked, too, and they understood. I was crushed when I didn't have to explain it, when they told me they knew the women had been raped, that they could see it. None of us needed more evidence than what we saw to know what we were looking at.

I wished I could look away. I wanted to hide it from my children, but I didn't dare. If I won't look, who will? If my children don't know what happened, who will?

"What can happen to a woman in nine months?" one of my friends at the table said, again. None of us had touched our food. I felt guilty for that, too. We were sitting in a synagogue, safe, with plates of food. What do the hostages have? Where are they?

You have to live. My great-aunt and grandparents used to tell me that when I was little. Over and over. *Survive.* It was an order, a way of life. I took a bite of my bagel.

"If there's a baby . . . there has to be a baby, right?" one friend said. She shook her head, wiped away a tear. "Who will love that child?"

It was a question you can ask only when you are with people you love and trust. Of course every child deserves love, but who will hold a child born to a hostage, and feed them, kiss them, comfort them? That's what she was asking. I didn't want to think about it, but I had to. If I don't think about it, who will?

What can happen to a woman in nine months?

In nine months in America, you can make dreams come true. You can graduate, get a job, marry, or have a child. You can make choices that will change the rest of your life. In nine months, if you're a hostage in Gaza, the unthinkable can get worse. Why isn't the entire world listening? What can happen to a woman in nine months?

RACHEL BARENBAUM is the author of the critically acclaimed novels *Atomic Anna* and *A Bend in the Stars*. She is a prolific writer and reviewer. Her work has appeared in the *Los Angeles Review of Books, Harper's Bazaar,* and more. She is the founder and host of the radio show *Check This Out,* a literary show that airs on NHPR.

PART FIVE

Jewish Mom-Life

Lihi Lapid

To Be an Israeli Mom

To be an Israeli mom is to see how your fetus (already, when the doctor says "It's a boy") grows to be a soldier in uniform, with road dust in his hair, a rifle on his shoulder, and his eyes full of innocence. And to start being worried.

To be an Israeli mom is to teach your daughter not to show weakness in front of her third-grade classmates, because she will have to be strong in front of her tough commander at age eighteen.

To be an Israeli mom is to complain about your country quite a bit, but always tell your children it's the best place in the world.

To be an Israeli mom is to be scared when the sirens go off, but to remember it's more important that your children don't stress out and aren't afraid, so you take a deep breath and tend to them first, like you are super-cool.

To be an Israeli mom is to be involved, to "consume" the news like a drug addict, to protest for or against, and always feel responsible for what's going on here, because it's yours. It's your state, and it's your children that will protect it. And to know that you don't have the option to be indifferent, not in this country. And, sometimes, to agonize that you didn't protest more.

To be an Israeli mom is to know about the situation no less than the chief of staff. And if you meet him, let him know what *you* think should be done.

To be an Israeli mom who lives by the border, near Gaza in the south or near Lebanon in the north, is to be part of a chain of wonderful brave Israeli women, for whom guarding their homes means guarding their country. And to hope this time will be the last.

To be an Israeli mom is to see uniforms hanging on the laundry rope, and to know that the mother or father who will fold them might shed a small tear and say a prayer that comes from deep within their heart.

To be an Israeli mom is to look at photos of our killed soldiers and try *not* to think about how much they look like your own son. And to think about it anyway.

To be an Israeli mom these days is to see a bereaved mother and feel her sharp pain in your chest, to run out of air. It's to know that that bereaved mother is not someone else; she is a mom exactly like you. And that it could have been you. To feel you are soul sisters, and hurt with her. To want to hold and hug her, but at the same time know you will never be able to actually ease her pain, and that there are no words.

To be an Israeli grandma is not to believe that both your grandson and granddaughter are being drafted to the army. After all, you were the one who told their grandpa, when he went to war, that by the time you had grandchildren this would end. And to wonder whether it will ever end.

To be an Israeli mom is to know that all you want to give your children is security, and to realize that this is the one thing you cannot actually promise them. And still know for a fact that Israel is the best place for your child. (I know this cannot really be explained to anyone who is not an Israeli.)

To be an Israeli mom is to want peace, but not be willing to give up safety or security. It's to get through the current month in Israel and to know that an Israeli mom deserves to grow her children quietly. It's also to know that one day peace and safety will come.

Because peace is the promise of the Israeli mother. And even if it looks so far away now, trust her. It will come. Because being an Israeli mom is to be someone that never, ever gives up.

LIHI LAPID is an author, journalist, and activist. She has written three bestselling novels: *On Her Own, Secrets from Within,* and *Woman of Valor,* as well as a bestselling children's book. For over ten years, Lapid has written a weekly column in the Israeli newspaper *Yediot Ahronot.* Those columns were included in a collection titled *I Can't Always Be Wonderful.* Prior to becoming a writer, Lapid was a professional news photographer. She lives in Tel Aviv with her husband, Yair Lapid, former Prime Minister of Israel, and their two children. She is the president of SHEKEL, Israel's leading organization for inclusion of people with disabilities.

Alli Frank

Today You Are a Woman, Tomorrow You Go to Summer Camp

T his summer my youngest daughter became a bat mitzvah, the centuries-old tradition of becoming a woman under Jewish law. To prepare, she spent days mastering her Torah portions, designing a mitzvah project aligned with her talents as a budding pastry chef, and contemplating her relationship with Judaism. Many an evening was frittered away in an exhaustive online search for the "perfect" floral dress and gold sandals to match the tallit she'd chosen with her grandmother.

Observing my daughter enthusiastically take on her bat mitzvah year of study, often at the expense of hanging out with friends or missing ski team practice, was both joyous and fraught. There are three unofficial responsibilities as the parent of a child preparing for their bat mitzvah—drive your child to Hebrew lessons, plan the ceremony and post-party, and deliver a rousing speech at the end of the service. Two were easy: Our Hebrew teacher lived within biking distance, and, with clear instruction from my meticulous kid, the party planning was a breeze. But what should I say to a Jewish girl, stepping into womanhood post–October 7 and post–*Roe v. Wade*?

Here's what I came up with.

Today you are a woman. Tomorrow you go to summer camp. As your mother I marvel at the hardworking, dedicated young woman that you have become, while continuing to hold on fiercely to the goofy, snow-sports-loving, cookie-baking, volleyball-playing, friend-embracing, laser-focused child that you continue to be.

I desperately want to be able to tell you that there is no greater time in the history of our country, our world, to step into womanhood. But I can't. You are aware enough of the current dynamics in the United States and in the Middle East to know that. I hope the following will at least provide you with a road map to create a better world for women and Jews than the one we find ourselves in today.

1. Read. Not social media, not unapologetically biased news, not omnipresent sound bites. Books. Be a beacon of knowledge and facts on what it is to be Jewish. The Torah is a great first book for you to start with, but the text is old and it can sometimes be challenging to find a modern connection. You have also read a handful of books on the Holocaust for school. These can provide context for what it means to be a Jew. However, I also want you to understand what being a Jew means in between these two paramount moments that tend to define how others see us. Read Leon Uris's Exodus, *a fictional account of the founding of the state of Israel. It's a page-turner. Thumb through* The Book of Jewish Food *by Claudia Roden. To be Jewish is to eat and to nourish the souls and stomachs of those you love. If you want to learn how* to be an irrepressible Jewish woman, read My Life by Golda Meir. And if you want your Jewish knowledge served up with a giggle, dive into The Big Book of Jewish Humor. Jews, despite surviving more tragedy than any one group deserves, have maintained their sense of humor; we are a funny people. By reading, you'll be able to share your values, traditions, and history with non-Jews from a place of knowing, of thoughtfulness. That is what we need most in the world right now: understanding.

2. Say yes. We are living in a time when being Jewish might feel like something to hide, to not draw attention to. You might be tempted to avoid going to certain places or doing certain things because of who you are. I do not want that for you. I don't want you cowering from the world because you are Jewish. I want you to say yes to every opportunity that comes your way. I want you to say, "Yes, I am Jewish and I am proud to be." I want you to embrace others who may have misconceived notions of what it means to be Jewish, and I want you to feel a responsibility to help them expand their knowledge. We are living in a world where too many people are saying no to those who are different than they are, no to expanding their minds. Be a yes person in a world of nos.

3. Do the hard thing. Your Jewish ancestors around the globe have been doing the hard thing for millennia. If they hadn't, we wouldn't be here. But against all odds, here we are. I want you to carry on that proud, fighting tradition. It's easy to be a coward. It's hard to stand up for what's right. It's easy to join in groupthink and action. It's hard to stand alone. It's easy to say, "Well, it's okay one more time." It's hard to say, "Never again." Knowing what's right is not hard. Acting on it is. Be a person of action for women's rights, for Jewish rights, for human rights.

4. Remain hopeful. Hopeful people are more likely to take positive actions and to view challenges as opportunities. You are coming into womanhood at a time when there are hurdles to female body autonomy and to embracing Jewish identity. These are challenges I did not have to contend with, and for that I am truly sorry. My generation was not able to resolutely protect yours. But the good news is that tides shift, change is inevitable, and you have the power to shape the future. If you are hopeful, if you say yes to opportunities, if you step up and do the hard things, and if you read and continue to educate yourself on the persevering lineage that you are fortunate enough to be a part of, you will become a force for positive change in this world. That is the best reason of all to celebrate being a Jewish woman.

ALLI FRANK has worked in education for more than twenty years. A graduate of Cornell and Stanford University, Alli lives in Sun Valley, Idaho, with her husband and two daughters. She is the coauthor with Asha Youmans of *Tiny Imperfections, Never Meant to Meet You, The Better Half,* and *Boss Lady,* and an essayist in *Moms Don't Have Time to: A Quarantine Anthology.*

Shirin Yadegar

A Mother's Fight

Fleeing Iran with my family was a decision born out of desperation, a leap into the unknown, grasping for safety amid the rising tide of antisemitism. As a Jewish Iranian woman, my mother sought sanctuary for my brother and me in the United States. Becoming a mother of four daughters, I always thought my girls would grow up free from the shadows of hatred that had darkened my homeland. Yet the events since October 7 have stirred the embers of old fears, igniting a flame of sorrow and anxiety that wakes me at night.

My eldest daughter, Eden Yadegar, a junior at Columbia University, stood before Congress with a resolve that left me breathless. Her voice, strong and unwavering, testified to the surge of Jewish hate on college campuses. Watching her, my heart swelled with pride and trembled with fear. Pride in her bravery, her ability to stand tall against a wave of darkness. Fear for the dangers she faces in her unyielding quest for justice. Should we bring her home for her safety? Hire security to shadow her? Transfer her to another school? Her voice was and continues to be a beacon, illuminating the terrifying reality that Jewish students face daily—a reality that my other daughters know all too well.

Bella, my freshman at USC, had her mezuzah torn off her dorm door. She was jolted from sleep by the haunting chants of "Intifada revolution" outside her window. These acts of hatred are not mere vandalism; they are wounds inflicted upon her soul, attempts to erase her identity and silence her spirit. Each incident echoes with the same venomous intent that drove us from Iran, reminding us that no place is immune to the scourge of antisemitism.

My middle-schooler, Lily, came home one day with tears in her eyes, the image of swastikas graffitied on her school walls etched into her mind. For a child her age, these images are a brutal assault on her innocence. Seeing her struggle to understand why such malice exists in the world breaks my heart and stirs a deep-seated rage within me. It is a stark reminder that the hatred we fled from can rear its ugly head anywhere, even in the supposed safety of American schools and culture.

Camille, my eleven-year-old, saw and heard the atrocities of October 7: babies burned alive, women raped and killed in front of their families. These horrors are too monstrous for any child to comprehend. She wrestles with nightmares about a world that seems both cruel and incomprehensible, while I grapple with shielding her from this harsh reality without hiding the truth. Her questions pierce my heart, each one a reminder of the innocence shattered by a world filled with hatred.

As a mother, my instinct is to shield my daughters, to envelop them in a cocoon of safety and love. Yet, as a journalist, I am driven to speak out, to shine a light on the darkness and give voice to those who are silenced. This balance has never been more precarious. The pain of seeing my children face the same hatred my family once fled is indescribable, but it fuels my resolve. I must be their pillar of strength, showing them that fear may grip us, but it cannot silence us.

Night after night, I wake in sweats, my mind plagued by the uncertainty of what tomorrow might bring. The fear and uncertainty for Jews in America gnaws at my peace, leaving me restless. In these dark hours, I find strength in my daughters' resilience and in my own voice. I stand on my platforms, not just as a mother, but as a warrior of words, amplifying the cries of our community, sharing the struggles of my daughters, and calling for justice and understanding. This is my daughters' generation's fight and I will be here to support and encourage their voices. We will not be silenced.

My journey is one of pain and fear, but also of courage and hope. As a mother, I strive to protect my children from the world's hatred while empowering them to stand tall and proud of their Jewish identity. Our story is a testament to the enduring spirit of those who, despite facing relentless adversity, continue to fight for their right to exist and thrive in peace. We are the voices that will not be silenced, the lights that refuse to dim.

SHIRIN YADEGAR is a mother, a journalist, a publisher and a TV host. Her magazine, *L.A. Mom Magazine,* and talk show *Moms Matter* have turned into a war room since October 7 in order to amplify the truth. Before becoming a mother, Shirin received her M.A. from USC's Annenberg School for Communication and Journalism and worked as a researcher and writer at the *Los Angeles Times* and as managing editor of *Beverly Hills Weekly*. Shirin currently serves on the boards of WIZO, Shero's Rise, and Visionary Women.

Anna Ephron Harari

When the Moon Broke Down

I wish there was a word for having a personal, suburban drama in the midst of a bigger world conflict. I wish there was a way to describe the guilt that coated every interaction and feeling I had throughout what happened.

It felt like I was trapped in a dream, a very specific dream I had more than a decade earlier. My ten-year-old Prius's engine had just failed. My subconscious absorbed this cosmic event, and that night I had a dream that the moon broke down. Black smoke billowed out and it fell from the sky. *I have to fix the moon,* I thought to myself. But the world had shifted upside down. The dream looked exactly like my normal life, but everything that was previously perceived as good was bad.

Sometimes I make quick assumptions about other people. First gen Prius = NPR liberal.

It isn't my best trait. Perhaps it's a protective mechanism I've developed; I wasn't always like that. Back in 2008, I went door to door for a presidential race in Alliance, Ohio. I had hour-long conversations with strangers. We rarely agreed, but we talked through our points and learned from each other. I wouldn't feel safe speaking to a stranger like this now. Was it a balloon of ignorance I lived in? Or has a balloon of hate spread so rapidly over the world, divided us so much, that we can no longer engage in conversation with someone we don't agree with? Somehow, I let myself slip into a "you're either with me or against me" mindset.

Last year, my daughter went to a progressive public charter elementary school that leased its campus from a conservative Jewish synagogue. My younger son attended the preschool at the synagogue. My daughter's teacher, who used they/them pronouns, defended their right to celebrate Pride at the school. That teacher was "with me." There were families at the elementary school who made subtle digs about their pronouns. They were "against me." There were families at the preschool who complained that Palestine was on the map in the classroom. They were "against me."

I was entirely unprepared for the whiplash this year at the same school.

By October 7, both my children were attending the elementary school. My daughter had moved up a grade, no longer in that teacher's class, so we were one degree removed from the group of children who came home from their lesson plan, confused to learn that Israelis were keeping children in cages.

Two of the first-grade teachers, including the one I had thought was my ally, took it upon themselves to teach a lesson plan about the conflict in Israel and Palestine from an anti-Israel perspective, and then post about it on social media. The post included offensive language written over images of the school, including one unspeakable line I replay over and over in my head. They even included images of the children's homework that *included their names*. I would have been equally horrified had it been from an anti-Palestinian perspective. But instead of addressing the wrongs—teaching a non-age-appropriate lesson from a biased perspective, and posting about it on social media with offensive language and children's personal information—it turned into a political debate. It became about polarizing buzzwords, as if we could solve the Middle East conflict in a proxy war in the PTA.

One parent meeting ended with everyone storming out of the room in tears. Afterward I went up to the acting administrator, who was leading the meeting by herself with no agenda nor tools, and asked her why she was there alone.

"With such a divisive topic, don't you think you should have had help?" I suggested. "A team of moderators with sensitivity training, perhaps?"

She looked at me with the blankest expression and said, "I didn't realize it was going to get so divisive."

It felt like she was pranking me. I kept thinking of the scene in *Clueless* where Josh asks Cher why she looks confused and she says, "I thought they declared peace in the Middle East."

All of a sudden, everyone I had flagged as "with me" was *defending* the actions of this teacher. One mother claimed "the Jews are running the school," then asked me to meet her at the park for a playdate. The Rubin Report picked up the story. I went from being the liberal, secular one in the Jewish preschool to being championed by conservative news pundits.

Every night as I tried to fall asleep, it felt like my head was spinning, as if I were drunk. My center of gravity had completely toppled over. I was living in that upside-down universe from my dream. Everything looked the same, and yet, everything was different.

I felt sandwiched between hysteria and gaslighting. I couldn't find my footing. In the subsequent weeks at school, one child got up in front of his class and announced, "I'm going to kill all the Jews." Another mother came to his defense, saying that her son "says things he doesn't mean all the time, like 'I'm going to kill this bagel.'" Then the families decided she was being antisemitic because of her word choice of "bagel."

But it wasn't the use of the word "bagel" that was antisemitic; it was the minimizing of what the child had done.

I called a rabbi at a different temple for counsel. He had officiated our wedding and our children's baby-naming ceremonies, but at first I hadn't thought to consult him; I was sure he had more pressing problems to handle. I asked if we could set a meeting. He called me ten minutes later. We spoke for an hour, honoring what I was feeling. Then he suggested I apply to his temple's elementary school. I felt like someone was listening to my problems but also saying, "I'm not minimizing that you are upset, but you also seem hungry. Eat."

I hesitated to switch schools, reluctant to send my kids to an all-Jewish school. I didn't want to put them in a bubble of like-mindedness. I wanted them to be around people with different opinions. I wanted them to be challenged and I wanted them to challenge me. But I knew their school was showing its true colors. The potential new school was exhibiting kindness and prioritizing education through Jewish values.

We switched schools, and I found myself caught in the loving embrace of a community that supports me and does not always agree with me. Both my children are thriving at the new school.

At the first Shabbat service, I broke down in tears. The room had stopped spinning. I have woken up from the dream, but now I want out of the universe in which things are either "good" or "bad." I want to live in the meaning, the space between polarizing buzzwords.

ANNA EPHRON HARARI is a writer and producer. She lives in Los Angeles with her husband and two children.

Jacqueline Friedland

The Hora, Not the Horror

Anyone who has been to a Jewish wedding or bar mitzvah has probably seen the hora, a traditional Jewish dance where people form a circle, link arms, circle to the left, circle to the right, and maybe come to the middle for a quick, joyous jig to celebrate the special event.

By the fall of 2023, my husband and I had bar mitzvahed three of our four children. At our parties, these hora dance circles gradually transitioned from grandparent-appropriate rotational circles to something entirely different. Gone was the gentle twirling, and in its place arrived exuberant, raucous bouncing, spirited moshing, and enough cheering and jumping to rival a challenging sporting event. Picture grown men in dress clothes covered in sweat, women who can't remember where they've tossed their shoes, adults bogeying from atop each other's shoulders, and even a few bouts of crowd surfing. But most of all, there were smiles and hugs and so much joy that you could feel it seeping out of people's pores. (It wasn't just the sweat, I promise.)

We were supposed to celebrate our fourth child's bat mitzvah in November 2023, mere weeks after the atrocities of October 7. How could we dance and celebrate when our Israeli brothers and sisters were grieving and suffering the losses and kidnapping of their loved ones? How could we give our daughter the cheering and whooping she'd been waiting for for so long when the survival of our homeland was in question? Israel was at war, people were dying, and we thought it was okay to dance? It boggled my mind to consider.

Obviously the party we had hoped to throw in honor of our child reaching a Jewish milestone was not nearly the most important thing going on in the world. Far from it. But it was important to *us*, and we needed to figure out how to handle it.

As I mulled over the possibilities, I was reminded of when my husband and I got engaged in New York City—on September 10, 2001 (as in, the night before 9/11). How strange it was in the weeks after the attack against our nation to struggle with our feelings of happiness about our engagement, while also mourning the losses suffered by our city and our country. Our rabbi reminded us during *that* time that Judaism encourages the balancing of life's joys and sorrows, and also that it is a *mitzvah* (a good deed) to celebrate life's milestone events with joy. I understood then that I had been given permission to feel all the things, to let my happiness and sorrow exist side by side.

I began to feel comfortable with the idea of celebrating a bat mitzvah after October 7, to let our joy at our daughter's milestone exist alongside our pain from the atrocities, the war Israel was being forced to fight, and the alarming anti-semitism surrounding us in the U.S. I also began to realize that it was not only a privilege to celebrate our child's bat mitzvah, but also our duty. With Jews still being actively persecuted, how could we forsake an opportunity to elevate this moment of Jewish joy?

As we moved closer to the big day, I heard from friends and family who agreed that there was no choice but to celebrate the welcoming of another Jew into the adult community. We could not let evildoers rob us of even more than they already had. The advice from members of our community was adamant and unanimous: We must proceed.

One couple made an especially important impact on the event. These American friends of ours had bid goodbye to their son and daughter a few weeks earlier, as the two young adults traveled to Israel to help the IDF. One entered active combat in Gaza and the other, having recently finished her own army service as a lone soldier, returned to Israel to do everything she could to help. As a gift to our daughter, their family organized a pizza party for a unit of IDF soldiers in honor of our upcoming *simcha*. Not only that, but they got a video of the soldiers enjoying their pizza and wishing our daughter—by name—mazel tov on the occasion of her bat mitzvah. They thanked her for giving them a reason to enjoy the special treat and told her they hoped she would have "so much fun" at her bat mitzvah.

Many families show a montage at their child's bar or bat mitzvah, displaying pictures of the child with friends and family over the previous thirteen years. At our party, we also played a slideshow. But first we aired the video from the soldiers. The smiling faces and warm wishes from the soldiers gave everyone in the room permission to celebrate, and it was also a somber reminder that we must always balance our joy with our sorrows.

And so it turned out that at our party, we did dance the hora, in our usual over-the-top style, but with one crucial change. We unfurled two large Israeli flags and held them above ourselves as we danced, keeping Israel top of mind as we tried to hold on to the sacredness of our child's brief and ephemeral milestone.

JACQUELINE FRIEDLAND is the *USA Today* bestselling author of *He Gets That from Me*. A graduate of the University of Pennsylvania and NYU School of Law, she practiced as a commercial litigator in New York for as long as she could stand it. After a brief stint teaching legal writing at the Benjamin Cardozo School of Law in Manhattan, Jackie returned to school to earn her master's of fine arts from Sarah Lawrence College, graduating from the program in 2016. In addition to writing novels, she now regularly reviews fiction for trade publications and appears at schools and other locations as a guest lecturer. Her fifth book, *Counting Backwards*, will be released in 2025. When not writing, Jackie is an avid reader of all things fiction. She loves to exercise, watch movies with her family, listen to music, make lists, and dream about exotic vacations. She lives in Westchester, New York, with her husband, four children, and two very bossy dogs.

Amy Blumenfeld

The Silver Lining to Singing Off-Key

Amakeshift stage in the basement of a Brooklyn church is not typically where you'd expect to hear a ten-year-old girl belt out cantorial liturgy from the Sabbath morning service. And yet, there I was at my first (and last) audition reciting the Hebrew prayer, *Mimkomo hu yifen b'rachamim,* in front of two hundred aspiring, slack-jawed thespians.

My uncle, an actor, was attending an open casting call for a community theater production of *Gypsy* and asked if I'd be interested in trying out for one of the children's roles. I begged my parents for permission. They relented. I spent weeks rehearsing my audition song—"Tomorrow" from *Annie*—and mentioned the news to a few close friends, who proceeded to broadcast my impending big break throughout the halls of our Jewish day school in Queens.

I was more excited than nervous as my mother and I drove to the audition, but as soon as we took our seats and witnessed other hopefuls light up the stage, I panicked. Aside from a couple elementary school concerts, my résumé was limited to a single line of dialogue as "Candle #7" in a Hanukkah skit and dancing a solo clad in head-to-toe golden spandex as the shank bone at our grade's Passover seder. I knew the moment the production assistant called my name that this was *not* going to end well.

The room was silent as I struggled to recall the lyrics to "Tomorrow."

"How about the birthday song?" the director asked kindly. "Can you sing 'Happy Birthday'?"

No. My mind was blank.

"Really, anything will do," he encouraged.

And then, just as I sensed they were about to thank me for my time, a Hebrew hymn emerged from my mouth. It was the only melody I had on tap, and while the meaning escaped me, each word flowed effortlessly, albeit off-key.

Needless to say, I was not cast in that production of *Gypsy*, but the audition became one of the more formative and meaningful experiences of my childhood. It was the first time I was cognizant of instinctively turning to religion as a source of comfort in a time of need—something I would continue to do for the rest of my life. It was also the first time I realized that Judaism wasn't simply an activity on a calendar like building a sukkah in our driveway every autumn, marching up Fifth Avenue in the Israel Day Parade every spring, or ushering in a new week by smelling cloves and cinnamon sticks during havdalah when three stars appeared in the night sky. It was all of it combined. And it was all part of me. In a strange way, the audition helped me discover my voice.

Judaism infused the home in which I was raised and it is at the core of the one I have created as an adult. My husband and I sent our daughter to Jewish day school, we keep kosher, regularly travel to Israel, and continue the tradition of having Shabbat dinner every week with family. But while I have chosen a similar Jewish path to the one paved by my parents, I have made some tweaks.

I grew up hearing the story of my paternal great-grandfather, a world-renowned Orthodox cantor named Israel Schorr. In addition to leading a synagogue near his home in Czechoslovakia, he often performed with other cantors. In the 1920s, a wealthy congressman from New York was vacationing in Czechoslovakia and attended one of those concerts. The congressman's Harlem congregation was searching for a new cantor and he decided to foot the bill for Israel Schorr to travel to New York and audition by leading the high holiday services. Unlike mine, his audition was a success. The congressman subsequently paid for the cantor's wife and six children to gather up their belongings and board a boat to New York Harbor. That's how my family came to America. The majority of their relatives back in Europe were murdered by the Nazis. The cantor's voice saved us.

My grandmother, his fifth child, was eight years old when she sailed over. She was extremely bright and way ahead of her time. She questioned *everything*. Why did the boys go to yeshiva but not the girls? Why were men and women separated in shul? And while she remained a loving and dutiful daughter who cared for her ailing father who tragically passed away at a young age, she asserted her independence. Though it was a different timbre, she, too, had a strong voice.

Unlike many of her peers, my grandma was not a child bride. Instead, she chose to work during the day as a legal secretary and put herself through Hunter College at night. Had she been born in a different era, she would have undoubtedly become a lawyer. She met my grandfather, a letter carrier, when he delivered mail to her office. He wooed her by slipping boxes of Raisinets between the envelopes. They raised their two children—my dad and my aunt—in a culturally rich, secular home. They did not keep kosher, and Saturdays were like any other day of the week.

My father, however, was very close with *his* grandmother (the cantor's wife, my namesake). And when he got in trouble with his parents, my dad would escape to her apartment for the weekend. He absolutely loved spending Shabbat with her—going to shul, grabbing fistfuls of cookies at the kiddush, and getting to know the religious world against which his own mother had rebelled. My father, who attended public school in Brooklyn, saw his cousins getting a yeshiva education and grew jealous. He yearned to understand Hebrew, to study Torah and Talmud. And so, years later, when he met my mom and started a family, they kashered their kitchen, enrolled my brother and me in day school, and immersed all of us in a tightly knit synagogue with shared values. In fact, it was this community that inspired my first novel, *The Cast.*

L'dor v'dor, from generation to generation, is a common refrain in Judaism. It can be found in many places—the Torah, Psalms, Siddur—and, recently, on an endless loop in my mind as I prepare for my daughter's first year of college. Like generations before, she has found a voice all her own. It is gentle, kind, steady, yet beautifully bold. My prayer for her, for the next generation, for the Jewish people, and for the world at large, is precisely what I sang that day in the basement of the church, except now I have the benefit of understanding the words. *Mimkomo hu yifen b'rachamim* means "from His place may He turn with compassion."

Perhaps that is what will heal our world: voices from different places filled with compassion.

I think we could all use some *rachamim* right now.

AMY BLUMENFELD is an award-winning author and journalist. She is a graduate of Barnard College, Columbia University, and received a master's degree from the Columbia University Graduate School of Journalism. Her articles and essays have appeared in various publications, including the *New York Times*, HuffPost, and *O, The Oprah Magazine*, as well on the cover of *People*. Amy's debut novel, *The Cast*, was selected as a *New York Post* Best Book of the Week. Her second novel, *Such Good People*, will be published in July 2025. Amy lives in New York with her husband and daughter.

Ilana Kurshan

Around the World in Forty Days of Preschool

My son's preschool class has been traveling around the world this summer. His teacher, who is endlessly creative, told her class of four-year-olds that every day they would fly in an airplane to a different country. She arranged all the chairs into rows with an aisle down the center, affixed a "seatbelt"—a ribbon taped to the back of the chair, which the kids would pull over their chests—and chose a different child each day to sit alone in the front wearing a pilot's hat. The teacher, who is also the flight attendant, hands out the children's lunchboxes while they are seated and flips over the "fasten your seatbelt" sign on the wall whenever anyone needs to get up to go to the bathroom.

I trust my son is not the only one who wakes up every morning bursting with excitement, eager for me to remind him, "Wait, which country am I flying to today?"

Thus far my son and his classmates have been to Italy, where they ate popsicles and called them "gelato"; Greece, where they played in inflatable pools in the preschool playground; and Holland, where they all brought their bicycles and helmets from home and rode around the schoolyard. My son tells me it is the most fun summer he has ever had, and I want to smile with a heavy heart. I wonder how long his blissful and endearing innocence can be sustained.

My son, though he is still only four years old, is not completely innocent. He knows that we are living in a country at war. Half the kids in his class have parents who have been away from home for long stretches—weeks or even months—for reserve duty. Two class parents serve in the military police, and when they drop off their kids in the morning, they are always in uniform.

Even though we live in Jerusalem, which is relatively safe compared to the rest of Israel, we have had emergency sirens and red alerts and he has had to huddle with his older siblings in our "safe room" at times when we, his parents, were not even home.

The other day, my son asked me if someone could invent a bathroom on wheels.

"Why?" I asked curiously.

"That way, if there's a siren while I'm on the toilet, I could just roll the whole bathroom away from the bad guys and not have to get up in the middle."

Every night he wakes with another dream about the "bad guys"—they infiltrate his home, his classroom, and his consciousness. And yet miraculously, in spite of it all, his preschool teacher has managed to create the illusion that he and his friends are spending the summer happy-go-lucky, traveling the world.

In reality, not many Israelis are traveling abroad this summer. Those who are not serving in the reserves likely have children who are, or friends with children who are off at war.

"Pray for my son, he is going into Gaza tomorrow," a friend texts me.

Instead of responding—what could I say?—I bake her challah for Shabbat, along with an extra loaf to give to a friend who is collecting homemade challah to deliver to soldiers. And yet we are the lucky ones. Some Israelis are still in hell, waiting and working desperately for the return of loved ones whose photographs are plastered across roadsides and billboards: BRING THEM HOME NOW. Others are in mourning, paralyzed by grief. Still others think that even if they could travel, where would they go?

Our world, unfortunately, has become increasingly inhospitable to Jews. My American friends and family report that armed guards have become a familiar sight outside synagogues and Jewish schools, though it's difficult for me to imagine. My husband, who was supposed to travel to Norway for an academic conference, was disinvited along with all his Israeli colleagues the same week that Norway, Ireland, and Spain recognized Palestine formally as a state. And my son tells me he is flying with his preschool class to Turkey, the same day that I read on the news about an Israeli plane that had to make an emergency landing in Antalya to evacuate a passenger in need of medical attention, only to discover that Turkish authorities refused to allow the plane to refuel.

I'm grateful that my son—who would never think to leave the house without a yarmulke on his head and ritual fringes hanging out from beneath his T-shirt—still believes that he can go anywhere in the world. I hope times will have changed by the time he is old enough to know better.

My husband and I are both American born. Making our home and raising our kids in Israel was a conscious choice.

We wanted them to grow up in an environment where Jewish culture is the national culture—where the streets of their neighborhood are named for the twelve tribes of Jacob, billboards advertise classes taught by local rabbis, and the supermarkets feature the special foods for the upcoming Jewish holiday. Our older kids attend the local public school down the block, where they pray every morning and study Bible and rabbinic literature alongside math and science. And yet all my kids are acutely conscious that the right to live as a free people in this land is not something we can take for granted. It is both a tremendous privilege and a weighty responsibility to live as Jews in the Jewish State.

I don't think my jet-setting preschooler would agree, but if I could fly anywhere in the world, there is nowhere I would rather be than home.

ILANA KURSHAN is the author of *If All the Seas Were Ink.*

Emily Tisch Sussman
The Twenty-Nine Nights of Hanukkah

G rowing up as a Reform Jew with a somewhat secular outlook, I hadn't really considered my Jewish identity to be a significant part of who I was. In the community where I lived, *everyone* I knew was Jewish, so it didn't feel particularly special or important. Our traditions were there in the background, but they weren't something I actively focused on or felt the need to emphasize in my daily life.

Everything changed when I had children. Becoming a parent made me reflect deeply on the experiences and values that were meaningful to me and what I wanted to pass along to my kids. One of the most cherished memories from my childhood was celebrating Hanukkah. I remembered fondly the joy of lighting the candles, singing the traditional songs, and feeling a part of something larger than myself.

When my two children were born just eighteen months apart, it turned my world upside down. Suddenly, I was navigating life with a two-year-old and a six-month-old while trying to maintain a career I had worked so hard for. The chaos and demands of parenting were overwhelming, and in the midst of it all, I realized that I hadn't even celebrated Hanukkah properly with them yet. It was time to reconnect with my heritage and share it with the kids.

The next year, in true busy mom fashion, I was late organizing the Hanukkah celebrations—about three days into the holiday—but I decided to jump in and celebrate anyway. We lit the candles each remaining night and sang the traditional songs. To my surprise and delight, the kids absolutely loved it. They were captivated by the flickering lights, the melodies of the songs, and the sense of togetherness that the rituals brought. Seeing their excitement and joy made me realize how important these traditions were, not just for me, but for us as a family.

By the time we reached the eighth and final night of Hanukkah, I felt a pang of regret for the early nights we'd missed. So I decided to extend our celebration and add those missed nights onto the end. Why not? It felt natural to keep going because the experience was so special and meaningful.

Somehow, we ended up celebrating Hanukkah for twenty-nine days straight. It was an extraordinary time, filled with laughter, learning, and bonding. My kids learned the songs, we talked about the stories behind the holiday, and we enjoyed the simple yet profound act of lighting the candles together each night.

The extended celebration of Hanukkah was a beautiful and transformative experience for all of us. It wasn't just about the ritual itself, but about the connection we were building and the cultural heritage we were embracing. My children's enthusiasm and genuine love for the traditions reignited my own connection to my Jewish identity. I found immense joy and fulfillment in sharing these moments with them and seeing them embrace and celebrate our heritage with such open hearts.

Soon, I began to see myself not just as a parent, but as a Jewish parent. This identity became an integral part of how I approached raising my children. I wanted them to grow up with a strong sense of who they were and where they came from, and to appreciate the richness of our cultural and religious traditions. We started incorporating more Jewish practices and celebrations into our lives, and each one brought its own unique joy and meaning.

I'm grateful for the journey that led me to rediscover and embrace my Jewish identity. It has enriched our family life in countless ways and provided a strong foundation of values, traditions, and memories that my children will carry with them throughout their lives. Celebrating Hanukkah for twenty-nine days was a turning point, a time when I fully realized the beauty and importance of our heritage, and one that continues to shape and inspire our family every day.

EMILY TISCH SUSSMAN is the creator and host of the award-winning iHeart podcast *She Pivots*, a Tony-nominated producer, a co-owner of the New York Giants and Gotham FC, and a mother of three. Emily created *She Pivots* after leaving her fast-paced job as the vice president of campaigns at the largest democratic think tank in Washington, D.C. Emily has made more than 250 appearances on MSNBC, CNN, Fox News, HLN, and CBS, and has contributed to publications such as *Parents* magazine, *Marie Claire*, *Bustle*, *SheKnows*, and HuffPost.

She has produced Broadway hits including *Shucked* and *How to Dance in Ohio*. She is a founding member of her local Moms Demand Action chapter and has served on the board of the Ethical Culture Fieldston School and the Ross School. She is a member of the Artists Council at the Whitney Museum of American Art and the Director's Circle at The Church. She is a member of the New York Bar and earned her J.D. from the Benjamin N. Cardozo School of Law.

Jeanne Blasberg
Conversion Lessons

I converted to Judaism twenty years ago. It wasn't in preparation for a wedding; I'd already been married fourteen years. I had settled in my husband's hometown of Boston, and had even begun rooting for the Red Sox, which, at the time, seemed like a bigger allegiance shift than becoming Jewish. His family wasn't religious, but the two of us wanted our children to have a clear religious identity. I dutifully drove carpool to Hebrew school several times per week, partaking in and enjoying each activity that required parental attendance.

One afternoon I took the rabbi aside and asked what the conversion process entailed. He rattled off the dozen or so requirements mandated by our temple and then tilted his head in curiosity.

"Why? Who wants to convert?" he asked.

"Me!" I said, feeling the weight of the answer.

I had been curious, but asking out loud—to the rabbi, no less—meant I would be going through with it.

"You?" he replied.

"Yes, me," I said a little more sheepishly, worried I was for some reason disqualified. Was it my blue eyes? My blond hair?

He laughed.

"You are one of the most devoted Jewish mothers in this congregation. I had no idea you weren't Jewish!"

I could have slipped under the radar after that. But then I would have missed two years of study with him. (We were on a slow conversion track, taking breaks during the summer, and then the rabbi and his wife had twins.) I would have missed traveling to Israel with my family as a capstone event and competing in the Maccabiah Games. My husband and I wouldn't have shared the closeness that came with leading our family's spiritual journey together. I would not have felt fully embraced by my temple community, nor would I have written the types of novels I do, inspired by the tradition of midrash. Becoming a Jew was one of the biggest and most important decisions of my life.

One afternoon in 2004, I told my father I was in the process of converting. He had intentionally eschewed religion, deriding it as the "pablum of the masses." If I really cared to, he'd said, I could choose my own religion someday. As he said this, I was a sixth-grader surrounded by Jewish friends preparing for bar and bat mitzvahs and Catholic friends going to something called CCD in preparation for confirmation. I felt like the only one without a connection to God.

Given my father's cynicism, I wasn't totally surprised when his reaction to my conversion journey was one of dismay. I expected his disdain to stem from his opinion of religion in general, but he asked, "Why would you convert to a religion that makes you and your kids a target of hate and violence?" I was struck silent by his tone, one I attributed to his not caring for my husband's family. Later, I would also interpret his reaction as one revealing his own prejudices as opposed to any real danger in the outside world.

I wasn't naïve. I was well aware that antisemitism existed, but in our well-educated northeastern enclave, I assumed it was in decline. Then again, it might have been pervasive, operating only under the surface, because twenty years ago, there was more decorum and civility concerning what was said in public. Hateful speech was not tolerated, and haters were forced to take cowardly and ignorant action under cover of darkness with spray paint and the like.

As I write this in 2024, however, the threat feels real. Our Jewish friends confide that they are stashing away liquid assets such as cash and gold in other countries for the day when they are forced to flee. Some are accumulating handguns to be prepared if the antisemitic mobs come to their door. A fellow student in a literature class openly derides Zionism as de rigueur. Our charming mountaintop Shabbat service must station a security guard on the ski-in access. The Israeli flag is removed from the door. When people can chant "Death to Jews" without any repercussions, and authors are blackballed and sidelined because of their Jewish identity or subject matter, it feels real.

As a convert, my mindset has always felt akin to a Passover lesson; every day, every hour, every minute we can make the choice to pursue freedom. I wake up every morning and choose my Jewish life. I choose to observe Shabbat, to study Torah, to help those in need, to welcome the stranger, to love my neighbor, and to read and write, inspired by great minds, including Jewish ones.

Being Jewish right now does not make me feel afraid as much as it makes me feel misunderstood. My religion, my spiritual home, is misunderstood. Judaism, the religion, is conflated with Zionism, the movement to establish a Jewish homeland, the history of which few "protesters" likely understand. Many Jews hold the ideals of Zionism dear while not agreeing with the tactics of the current Israeli government. I doubt many protesters have taken the time to understand the complexity of these things. That is what Hamas was counting on: for the world to not understand, for the world to rely on sound bites and social media.

Since the attacks last October, it has been comforting to spend time with other Jews, people who share the nightmare of trying to explain ourselves to intolerant ears that don't attempt to listen. Twenty years ago, I had the luxury of walking away from such a conversation, but being a Jew means staying put and speaking up.

So here I am.

JEANNE BLASBERG is a mother, athlete, and creator. Her third novel, *Daughter of a Promise*, was released April 2, 2024. She cochairs the Boston Book Festival and serves on the executive committee of Grub Street, a preeminent creative writing center in Boston. She is the CEO of Flynn Creek Farm in Verona, Wisconsin.

Elizabeth L. Silver

The First Pang

Whaten I was thirteen, a kid scribbled "I hate Jews and n#$%" all over my notebook in class a few months after we moved from New Orleans to Dallas. Thirty years later, though his name escapes me, I remember that day clearly. I showed my teacher the notebook with the hateful graffiti, and then I went home and asked my parents why they moved us to this neighborhood where I was essentially the only Jew and there were no other minorities.

I was starting to learn how small a group of people we were, while simultaneously serving the role in my school community as one of the tokens. Nearly every week at lunch in the cafeteria, I was welcomed to join various Christian youth groups.

"But I'm Jewish," I would tell them.

"Oh, it's okay," they would reply, friendly with glistening smiles, as if just mentioning my Jewish identity was something that was maybe forgivable, a sometimes-acceptable wrongdoing, something I could—or *should*—try to escape by the good grace of their generous invitation. "We won't hold that against you. *Everyone* is welcome here."

Most of the students didn't seem to care about the fact that I was Jewish, but rather they looked at me as a novelty. Despite my secular life, I was something different, something mysterious, something they'd never previously seen. A *Jew.*

A few days after the graffiti incident, the kid came over to my locker, his head hung low, his brown hair falling onto his brow so that he didn't have to really look me in the eyes, and said the words he was told to say.

"I'm sorry."

"Thanks," I said, and then I never saw him again.

I don't know if he stayed at the school or left, if his family moved, or what really happened to him, but I never forgot that apology: quiet, demure, face down, his eyes disconnected from the intended recipient.

It was my very first pang. Most Jews feel their first one at some point. A reminder that you are different, not quite a part of the rest of the world.

I didn't think it would happen for my kids in elementary school, but this year when my ten-year-old daughter, the lively, friendly, empathic, overflowing-with-confidence theater kid with the clearly Jewish name, was in fourth grade at her Los Angeles public school, it happened.

March is both Asian American and Pacific Islander (AAPI) Heritage Month *and* Jewish American Heritage Month (JAHM). My kids' excellent public school was celebrating AAPIs and learning, rightly so, about AAPI history in and out of class. Some of my daughter's classmates voluntarily gave wonderful presentations about their families' countries of origin. She came home for the first few weeks of the month excited, telling me stories that she'd learned from her friends and classmates. Then, one day she came home a bit nervous and asked to quickly google something.

I watched as she scrolled, the glint of the screen reflected in her investigative eyes.

"No!" she said, near breathless, clarity materializing before her.

She showed me. March, she had just then realized, was *also* Jewish American Heritage Month, and her school had inadvertently neglected to acknowledge this. It wasn't that there was a problem with discussing cultural appreciation months; rather, it was that the school had done so for every other culturally identified month *except* her own.

A few days later just before bedtime, she came to my husband and me in her pajamas, her face washed with patches of red, her eyes sore, her typically strong voice timid, almost scared.

"I really want to do a presentation on being Jewish for Jewish American Heritage Month, but I'm scared to," she said, the words stretched thin over a vast canyon. "I don't want people to think I'm stealing the spotlight from all of the other kids in my class who are celebrating AAPI month. I don't want to take up space."

She paused, looked away, and then looked back at us.

"Also . . ." she added, nervous. "My friend told me that other kids in the class might not want me to do it."

And there it was. Her first pang.

We talked about it with her. We told her that the school probably just doesn't know it's also JAHM, and that we could talk to her teacher about it if she wanted to do a presentation, too.

"No," she said, pausing. "I can ask her myself."

Later that night, we watched from outside her bedroom as her light stayed on till ten o'clock, till eleven, even till midnight. We knew exactly what she was doing.

The following morning, she was awake and at the breakfast table early, her school-issued Chromebook open beside her bowl of cereal, the PowerPoint already on slide six: famous Jews, just after her favorite holidays, foods, and family traditions, replete with sound effects, and songs, and graphics.

As I drove her to school, the pang that hit me when I was thirteen years old reignited. I didn't know how they would respond to her request and presentation. But when she came home later that day, proud and joyful, she told us that her teacher was so happy to have her give the presentation; she just hadn't known about the month. Many of her classmates, she said with a smile, told her with excitement that they'd even eaten latkes before, and loved them.

It reminded me not just of that moment in middle school when the boy defaced my notebook out of hate but also of every other moment where I, too, was mostly the anomaly. People would frequently say to me, "You're the first Jew I've met," without negativity or hatred but rather curiosity.

We forget how small a tribe we really are at 0.2 percent of the world's population. Despite our disproportionate societal output, we all become mini ambassadors to our existence, to our history, and to our culture. And while we don't individually represent an entire religion, culture, or people—who look largely like every race, many of whom don't practice religion at all—we do represent one tiny part of it. Talking about that can become one of our superpowers, spreading understanding, love, and acceptance across the globe.

ELIZABETH L. SILVER is the author of the novel *The Majority,* the memoir *The Tincture of Time: A Memoir of (Medical) Uncertainty,* and the novel *The Execution of Noa P. Singleton.* Her work has been called "fantastic" by the *Washington Post,* "masterful" by the *Wall Street Journal,* and "important" by the *Los Angeles Times* and has been published in seven languages and optioned for film. A graduate of the University of Pennsylvania, Temple University Beasley School of Law, and the University of East Anglia's creative writing M.F.A., Elizabeth has written for the *Washington Post,* the *Guardian, New York* magazine, *Harper's Bazaar, Los Angeles Review of Books, McSweeney's,* and others and currently teaches creative writing with the UCLA Writers Program. She is the founder and director of Onward Literary Mentoring and lives in Los Angeles with her family.

Keren Blankfeld

Reading Signs

T hey're at an age when they don't yet read the signs. This is good, I think. Throughout the fall, scrawled graffiti and makeshift bumper stickers on lampposts have been popping up along the bucolic Park Slope streets, signs I'd rather they not read.

The smaller one is three years old; his older brother is four. When I pick them up from school they're playing on the schoolyard roof, balls flying in the air, children climbing on monkey bars. It's getting cold, but they don't care. They wear short sleeves, with jackets and backpacks tossed on the asphalt ground, and they don't want to leave.

They're at an age when they ride their scooters from school, crunch golden maple leaves on the sidewalk, marvel at the three-legged dog hopping by, and wave at the man who holds the leash and pushes a baby stroller.

Sometimes they break into song. Their voices are not loud, but they sing without restraint these boys, still chubby-cheeked, eyes glimmering with discovery and glee, often eliciting smiles.

One day, when they sing in Hebrew, a Hanukkah song, I flinch and look around. They just learned this song at school, and they are proud they know the words, but their voices now seem much too loud. I tell them to lower their voices and am immediately ashamed of myself.

I wear a golden chain with a butterfly around my neck. The necklace belonged to my grandmother, who gave it to me decades ago. I wear it every day. That night, I look in the mirror and think of my grandmother, a blond-haired, blue-eyed Polish Jew who was sent on a ship of orphans to Palestine when she was seven years old. My grandmother, petite and strong-willed, told me about how they'd tried to keep her off the transport because she didn't "look Jewish." But already at seven she was stubborn. Already at seven she knew who she was.

"I am a Jew," she insisted, although in her world they killed Jews. Most of her family was already dead. With her persistence, off she went, a pale Jewish girl, to start a new life, growing oranges in a kibbutz.

A few days later, I find a Star of David and put it on a chain around my neck, joining my grandmother's butterfly.

At bedtime, I lie down on the rug in the space between my sons' toddler beds, a ritual that I know won't last, but that I'll hold on to for as long as possible. They ask for water, they ask for food, they ask to go to the bathroom. They talk, tell jokes, and sing quietly to themselves. I love the sudden questions, when I think they've already drifted off to sleep: "Why are our legs longer than our arms?" or "Did we come from monkeys?"

And then one night the oldest starts singing, softly, and I freeze. His voice gets louder:

. . . Od lo avdah tikvateinu
Hatikva bat shnot alpayim,
Lihyot am chofshi be-artzeinu,
Eretz tzion, virushalayim.

His brother joins him, and they sing Hatikvah on a loop, soft at first, then louder and louder. My eyes water, as we all lie in the dark. Soon they drift off to sleep.

A few days later, they sing Hatkivah on their scooters, on the way to school. My body tenses up, but this time I don't tell them to lower their voices.

Winter has come and gone. The spring days are glorious and golden. The graffiti on the lampposts has multiplied. I touch the butterfly and the star around my neck.

The graffiti ink will fade, I tell myself. The signs will disintegrate. And my children, their children, the Jewish people, will live on, as we always have: proud.

KEREN BLANKFELD is an award-winning journalist whose stories have appeared in the *New York Times, Smithsonian,* and other publications. Her first book, *Lovers in Auschwitz: A True Story,* is being translated into fourteen languages. Keren teaches journalism at the Columbia University Graduate School of Journalism. Originally from São Paulo, Brazil, Keren spent her teenage years in Houston, Texas. She now lives in New York with her husband and two sons.

PART SIX

Bling

Amy Klein

A (Jewish) Star Is Worn

"Are you *JEWish*?" the man on the subway shouts, staring at my chest.

To be fair, I am wearing a prominent silver Jewish star necklace.

It's not "Hebrew Hammer" bling, but as someone who has never worn any identifiably Jewish markers—no hamsa jewelry, "chai" tattoos, or even a yarmulke, as my brother and father do—I can feel the six-point silver star pulsing around my neck, inviting all of New York City to comment.

There has probably never been a worse time to start advertising my religion—not after the October 7 Hamas attacks on Israel, not when antisemitism in America went up more than 600 percent, according to the ADL, when college campuses around me became dangerous for Jews (I live near Columbia University), when posters of the kidnapped victims were getting defaced all around me on the Upper West Side and in Harlem.

But when a friend gifted me the necklace in December for helping her have a baby (I write about infertility), how could I say no?

My husband is a secular Israeli, with most of his family in Israel, and I'm a naturalized Israeli citizen, having lived there in my twenties. I'd made many close friends there: friends with kids in the army, friends with children displaced by the war, or, like one old acquaintance, the mother of a son in captivity whose desperate pleas on social media still give me daily nightmares.

How hard could it be to simply exist in America and wear a Jewish star?

"I *am* Jewish," I tell the man, moving to the back of the subway car, as my Krav Maga Israeli defense class instructor taught me. I'd joined the six-week training at a local synagogue (one that, as an ex-Orthodox Jew married to an atheist, I do not attend). The class was a compromise in this volatile city, as people around me were talking about buying guns. I'd already gone to a firing range with a former Israeli special ops officer, but decided that owning a gun wasn't for me. Not with a nine-year-old in the house. ("You can always escape to my bunker," the special ops guy told me.)

"Always be alert, NEVER wear headphones, and keep your back to the wall," my Israeli instructor said, while teaching us to throw kicks and punches, break a chokehold, and, worst-case scenario, knee them in the groin.

But the man talking to me isn't dangerous. Although he's missing a tooth and is two days short of a shower, he wants to talk to me about Judaism, about whether I believe in both the New and Old Testament. I would continue the conversation, but I've reached my stop.

"Sorry!" I say, glad that the interaction was anodyne.

I'm not so lucky a few days later, waiting in line to watch journalist Bari Weiss (*How to Fight Anti-Semitism*) at the 92nd Street Y on the Upper East Side, and a protester holds up a sign in my face that says "Nazi." My blood boils. I want to jump the police barricade, tear down the sign, and use some self-defense moves.

"Just ignore them," another woman in line says—which is what Jerry Seinfeld later does as he exits the talk, getting cursed at and called a genocide supporter.

Yet as winter turns to spring and I start to shed some layers—scarves, sweaters, and turtlenecks—I cannot ignore the looks my Jewish star gets, on the subway, at my coworking space, even in the dog park.

It's nothing overt. I am not on the train when keffiyeh-masked men take over a subway car, chanting, "Raise your hand if you're a Zionist! This is your chance to get out!" to round up Jews. *On. The. Trains.* I've not been doxxed on social media by the "Watermelon Brigade"—commenters who force Jewish content creators into hiding if they don't make a statement supporting Gaza. With our daughter attending a Jewish day school, I live in a relative bubble.

But I get looks. "Microagressions," as the kids call them, leaving me to wonder if each interaction—the traffic ticket, the refused entry to the city pool, the sneering waitress—is arbitrary or antisemitic.

I find myself twisting my necklace in public spaces, assessing the people around me—*Are they Jewish? Do they hate Jews?*—just like my Krav Maga instructor would like, but I don't like this feeling. This feeling of being unsafe in America. A Jew in New York.

I wish I could say I am standing proud. That I refuse to be cowed by a very loud minority. (Almost two-thirds of Americans view the Israeli people positively, according to a Pew poll.) That I will wear my Judaism proudly, like the religious men I know or the Israelis fighting for our country.

But I'm a mom. *Not that that's an excuse,* I think, remembering the moms of the missing. I'm just a woman worried about her safety.

So I swap out my silver star for a different necklace that I bought from an Israeli artist. It's a small gold rectangle, like the Israeli dog tags many Jews wear to symbolize support for the hostages. Instead of "Bring Them Home" inscribed in large letters, under the dotted line in the middle (where a dog tag is broken in half if a soldier dies), there's a tiny Jewish star. It's the kind of thing that you can see only if you're standing close—or if you're in the know. More than a few people have caught my eye and given me the Jewish nod, and I nod back, thinking, *I can't believe it's come to this.*

I hope that one day soon there will be peace, that our kidnapped will be returned—alive!—that the protesters in America will find another cause du jour, and that I will feel secure enough in America to put my big silver Jewish star back on.

AMY KLEIN has been covering the Jewish world for the last three decades, contributing to everything from CNN to the *Jerusalem Post*, the *Forward*, *Haaretz*, and *Hadassah Magazine*. She is the author of the book *The Trying Game: Get Through Fertility Treatment and Get Pregnant Without Losing Your Mind*, which is based on her successful *New York Times* "Fertility Diary" column, in which she chronicled her journey to have a baby (ten doctors, nine rounds of IVF, and four miscarriages in three countries).

Talia Carner

Flaunting My Star of David

A t the market checkout, the shopper ahead of me bags her groceries, and my glance hooks on the large gold chai hanging on her neck. She catches my eye, and her gaze travels down to my new Star of David. With delight on her face, she gives me a high-five. At that moment, we, two strangers, are united with double invisible strings: the gnawing worry about Israel under an existential threat and the rise of antisemitism in the U.S., which cause us both to flaunt the symbols of belonging to a proud tribe.

But there is a third layer of anguish I carry that I don't share with my transient soulmate: that of a Jewish author. And not just any Jewish author, but one singled out for an antisemitic attack.

It began on December 17, 2023, six weeks prior to the release of my novel, *The Boy with the Star Tattoo*, on January 30, 2024. A British influencer recorded two TikTok videos, calling her large following to review-bomb the novel and to compel my publisher to "deplatform" me. Her call for action immediately flooded my Instagram page with hateful comments. More prominently, it found fertile soil on Goodreads, where unchecked reviews can appear on a book's page as soon as it is listed, even months before its publishing date.

That day, the novel, whose advance reader's copy was available only to hand-picked bloggers and reviewers, saw a shower of one-star ratings and mostly anonymous text "reviews" on Goodreads by people who could not possibly have had access to the novel. They accused me of a variety of crimes of omission and action against Palestinians.

I will never know the hundreds of faceless, nameless Instagrammers and bloggers who jumped into the fray with enough five-star ratings to bring the average up to four stars, thus saving the novel before it had come out of the gate. But the one entity that remained unmoved while this battle was raging on its site was Goodreads. Despite my emails and the efforts by my publisher to point to Goodreads's own guidelines against harassment, the site's moderators steadfastly refused to remove the offending campaign. Even today, Goodreads continues to give these haters a place to drop more bombs on my novel.

But that wouldn't stop me. In the months that followed, embraced by the Jewish community and by literature lovers, I forged ahead with my book tour with fifty in-person events. Heeding an FBI agent's advice, I scheduled secured venues—synagogues, JCCs, and gated communities. No bookstores or libraries, where TikTok followers could show up with megaphones. I paid an internet service to remove my home address from all public records.

Yet all around me, fires were burning, as Jewish authors— often novices struggling to get a foot in the door—wrote to me about their woes. An agent canceled a contract with one author after having accepted her Jewish-themed novel. Another Jewish author hit a wall when trying to schedule bookstore readings for his new novel, released by a mainstream house.

That's when I bought my Star of David necklace, the first in my life.

The warm reception and healthy book sales within the Jewish community could not mask the fact that, released four months into the bloody Israel-Hamas war, my novel got no traction outside of it. For my previous novel, I had been interviewed by more than thirty podcasters, but this time I could count them on one hand.

The legendary suspense writer Nelson DeMille endorsed my book, writing, "Historical fiction doesn't get better than *The Boy with the Star Tattoo*," yet mainstream reviewers kept mum. Privately, one told me that the novel was "phenomenal," but he "didn't cotton the hailstorm" that a glowing review (of a pro-Israel book) would create. Read differently: He was intimidated.

Although each novel I'd written had brought me a wider circle of readers, I lowered my expectations for this book. I stopped posting book tour dates and locations on my website and social media.

Six months into the attack against my novel, while many news outlets have published accounts of antisemitism in the U.S. literary world—my case has had the dubious distinction of starring in some of these articles—something nagged at me. Why hadn't the Authors Guild, which represents more than 14,000 authors, released a statement against antisemitism directed at its members? In its mission, the AG states its clear objection to bias against authors and to banning books. It champions the rights of authors to earn a living in a safe environment. Yet, when I and others revealed on the AG's discussion board the antisemitic environment in which we found ourselves, our posts were removed and we received private warnings from the moderators. We were therefore barred from responding to vile anti-Israel posts on the same forum. (AG claims to have removed them, but it took days after our flagging them, while ours were struck instantly.)

Finally, I penned a letter to the board and staff, demanding that they take a public stand for us, Jewish authors, the way they had for authors of color. I made my letter public. It took the Authors Guild about ten more days before it issued a watered-down statement, wrapping antisemitism with Islamophobia—except that there is no known campaign to blacklist Muslim authors.

What's next?

While my team has had my back, the overarching atmosphere calls for a joint statement of all major publishing houses to dispel the impression that agents who turn down Jewish authors do so as the gatekeepers to the acquisition editors' preferences. Together, U.S. publishers must force Goodreads to apply its own antiharassment and anti–hate speech policies and compel the site to stop providing a platform for Jew haters.

I am taking the summer off to start writing my seventh novel, which is neither Jewish- nor Israeli-themed. My book tour for *The Boy with the Star Tattoo* will resume in the fall with more talks within the Jewish community, where I will flaunt my Star of David but otherwise be silenced by hatred.

TALIA CARNER is an award-winning author of six novels and numerous articles. Her historical and psychological suspense novels bring to the forefront indignities and human dramas long ignored. Most recently, inspired by the rescue of Jewish orphans post–World War II and weaving it into the Israel navy's 1969 story of ingenuity and daring, she wrote *The Boy with the Star Tattoo*. Talia lives in New York and Florida.

Abby Stern

I Refuse to Quote Coco Chanel

"Style is something each of us already has, all we need to do is find it."

—Diane von Furstenberg

Most people who encounter me in the wild—frazzled, running errands, and doing daily chores—would be surprised to learn that I love fashion. I *am* aware that the monotonous black-on-black athleisure I've dubbed "my uniform" isn't fashion. But even in my stretchy-clothes-security-blanket era, I sneak in some personal style with accessories, mostly jewelry. Despite being dressed similarly and sometimes identically to other blond women in practically every age demographic in Los Angeles, my jewelry gives me a sense of identity. As the cliché says: Style shows people who you are without speaking. So, clasped and hooked daily are my staples: gold hoop earrings of varying thickness and diameter, a diamond tennis bracelet my best friend generously gifted me for my fortieth birthday, and at least two different gold necklaces, layered.

One necklace I don't own or wear is a Star of David.

"You don't look Jewish."

I hear this from almost every new acquaintance when the subject comes up. They glance at my neck to see if they missed clocking the necklace that would announce my religion. Then the squinting begins, attempting to analyze my features to discover a clue they'd missed. You see, I look like a shiksa (a gentile woman). I've never taken offense at others' surprise. In fact, I'm starting to think that my lack of external Jewish identification, though subconscious, has perhaps been intentional.

I was familiar with the term "generational trauma." Always the skeptic (I've watched way too many cult documentaries where these types of terms are used to indoctrinate followers), I assumed it was psychobabble. But on October 7, 2023, I realized how wrong, dismissive, and arrogant I'd been. The feelings of fear, anger, loss, self-preservation, and a nightmarish déjà vu were inescapable. Once I felt them, I knew on a cellular level they'd always been there but had been dormant.

So, I wondered, if generational trauma *is* real, perhaps survival instincts are also ingrained in us. My blond hair and blue eyes genetically came from my grandma Jean. This aesthetic curried an enormous amount of favor and a small yet penetrable layer of protection for her as a girl in Poland. She worked at a shop owned by fellow Jews. When the tides began turning in Eastern Europe, she was tasked with working at the front of the store *because* of her non-Jewish-looking features.

"Is this store owned by Jews?" Nazis would come in and demand to know.

"No," she replied with an unfathomable, unshakable composure. That, coupled with her Aryan looks, was enough for the Nazis to walk back out again. For the time being.

Being Jewish is a part of me but it has never felt like one of the major threads in my overall identity. Growing up, I did all of the Jewish things. I went to Sunday School at the temple through confirmation. I was bat mitzvahed at age thirteen. I went to what we so affectionately refer to as sleep-away "Jew camp" from first grade through sixth grade. I sang the songs, I went to services, I learned the traditions. I even went on the Birthright trip to Israel as an adult. Still, none of these activities tripped some sort of Jewish engagement wire for me. I was perfectly fine being Jewish at a superficial level. I felt safe.

But on October 7, 2023, the wires were tripped and everything changed. I'm still trying to figure out what *truly embracing my Jewishness* looks like. Some things may change, but I'm still me. I won't be going to services or lighting the Shabbat candles. But a Star of David necklace just might make an appearance in my daily jewelry rotation.

ABBY STERN has almost twenty years of experience working as a writer and reporter. She has contributed to *People* magazine since 2007 and specializes in writing about entertainment, fashion, beauty, and other lifestyle content. She holds a B.A. in theater from the University of Southern California, where she was a film critical studies minor. Her writing has been published in *People, Entertainment Weekly, InStyle,* Yahoo, The Zoe Report, Poosh, and FabFitFun, among others. Abby's debut novel, *According to a Source,* was published to rave reviews. Goop called it "a fast, witty book with a dose of gravitas."

Jamie Brenner

Showing My Hand

G rowing up on Philadelphia's Main Line, my mother and grandmother would no sooner leave the house without wearing jewelry than they would without wearing shoes. I can still picture my grandmother's oversized gold coin necklace, ropes of turquoise, the delicate bangle bracelets and wide silver cuffs. My eighty-year-old aunt wears a T-shirt that reads "Whoever dies with the most jewelry wins."

When I turned ten years old, my grandparents gave me a necklace from Israel: a hamsa charm. It had a delicate gold filigree design and a tiny blue Star of David in the center. They told me its meaning: The hamsa is an ancient Jewish symbol of luck and protection. At that age, I was still blissfully innocent about the weight of my Jewish heritage. I was a happy child, and my Judaism was a source of pride. The hamsa was beautiful and appreciated, but I already felt lucky and protected.

I wore the hamsa necklace for a few years, but by the time I was a bat mitzvah it was replaced by Madonna-inspired rhinestone chokers and handmade beaded friendship neck-laces. The hamsa was relegated to my heart-shaped ballerina jewelry box.

After college, I moved to New York City, where minimal-ism was de rigueur. My boss wore only a single strand of pearls. To me, she was the ultimate New Yorker, the ultimate book person, and my new style icon. For the first time in my life I actively wanted a specific type of jewelry, and it was a string of pearls. It would take me five years to acquire them.

Fast-forward twenty years. I'm a published novelist. I'm still wearing pearls daily. But I'm older now, more interested in expressing myself. I add costume jewelry to the mix, mostly charms from designer Lulu Frost. And I realized that jew-elry, like books, has a narrative. It tells the world who we are. Around my neck, I wear a vintage subway token (New Yorker!) and a gold-plated ram figurine (Aries!), an oversized bronze-plated letter *J*. I wrote a book about a woman who turns vintage trinkets into necklace charms. My jewelry jour-ney is complete.

But on October 7, 2023, I'm reminded that I'm part of something much larger and more important than myself: I'm a member of the Jewish diaspora. In the days and weeks fol-lowing, when I walk around feeling more connected to Jew-ish strangers than I do to some of my closest friends, I yearn for a way to express this strange sensation. And it strikes me, in a moment of shame, that my jewelry is reflecting every-thing about myself except the most fundamental part: my Judaism.

The hamsa necklace is now forty-three years old. Unlike so many pieces in my collection, it is not chipped or tarnished or diminished in any way. Pulling it out of the soft cloth pouch where it has survived marriages and moves and the upheaval that comes with five decades of life, I wonder how I could have neglected it for so long.

As I write this, the hamsa hangs around my neck, where it will remain for the rest of my days. I'm proud to tell the world who I am, to show my hand. As a novelist, I know it's the most important story I'll ever tell.

JAMIE BRENNER is the bestselling author of eight novels, including *The Forever Summer* and *Blush*. Her latest book is *A Novel Summer.* Jamie grew up in suburban Philadelphia on a steady diet of fiction and soap operas, then moved to New York City, where she worked in book publishing and fashion. After raising two daughters in Manhattan, Jamie has returned to her hometown and spends her summers visiting the beaches that inspire her novels.

PART SEVEN

Am I a Good Enough Jew?

Caroline Leavitt

Good to Be Jewish, Even If I'm Not a Good Jew

When I was a kid, it wasn't good to be Jewish, especially when your family lived in an all-Christian Boston suburb. When I was in grade school, kids would routinely yell, "You killed Christ!" to me, or even dig their fingers into my curls to find the horns they knew were there. But back then, I didn't really understand what it meant to be Jewish, other than my mother's stories about growing up as an orthodox rabbi's daughter, her joy in her family's rituals and big communal table, the singing they did, the food they ate.

She gave it all up the day her beloved father died in Temple, because what kind of God would kill such a good man? But she never stopped yearning for that community, and she never tried to re-create it, either. I wasn't raised knowing about the holidays or the history. I didn't go to Hebrew school and never had a bat mitzvah, and the only Jewish thing we did was go to my grandmother's synagogue during the high holidays, which stopped when I was in fifth grade because my grandmother was too ill to go.

To me, being Jewish meant only one thing: You were an outsider.

But then I had a baby, a son. And it wasn't just about me or my husband anymore. We wanted our son to know who he was, to be able to decide later how much or how little Jewishness he wanted. And so, we had a bris. We opened our home to the ceremony. We hired a mohel, famous for planting gardens of foreskins of the babies in New York City. To my surprise, my mother and sister were not happy.

"A bris is barbaric!" my mother chastised me.

"Have a doctor do it. It's disgusting and hypocritical, because what kind of Jew have you been?" my sister said.

Making matters more complicated, the day of the bris, I was getting over a critical illness, sick in bed upstairs. My husband, Jeff, used the baby monitor so I could track what was going on downstairs. Everybody came—cousins, nieces, nephews, aunts and uncles, and friends, too—and I felt bathed in their joy and their love. Afterward, Max, our baby, was brought up to me so I could hold him and celebrate. Here he was, Jewish and in my arms, and I felt that connection like a lightning bolt.

We didn't push religion on Max as he grew up, but we made sure he read books and saw films about being Jewish. He especially loved Shari Lewis's *Shari's Passover Surprise.* (And so did I. We both sang all the songs while we watched it over and over again.) And it was Max who told us he wanted a bar mitzvah, and he wanted to invite his whole class. We hired a tutor for him, someone to make sure he knew what it meant to be Jewish, what the holidays meant, and what he would do and speak about the day he became a man.

Of course, my sister accused me of being a hypocrite again. "The money should go to his college fund," my mother told us. But we were busy opening our hearts. We held the ceremony and the party in a rock 'n' roll club and had karaoke and food with T-shirts as party favors.

I cried watching Max onstage. I cried when it was my time to speak, because I was so moved. I cried watching all the kids dancing and whooping it up, full of bliss and food. All that love, all that community, marking a special day in a boy's life, made me feel so grateful.

Some people might think we are not "good Jews" because we don't go to temple, we don't have Passover seders and we don't light candles for Shabbat. But for me, being Jewish is about more than the rituals. I feel that connection, that DNA handed down to me from my ancestors, including my grandmother, who escaped the pogroms, and my grandfather, who became a rabbi and was also a writer.

Maybe my mother never got back her orthodox Jewish childhood, but I put her stories into my novel, *Days of Wonder*, so readers could live the joy she had felt, too. So readers could understand.

My worship may not be in a temple, but it is now in every novel I write and the stories I tell, so that everyone who is not Jewish can live and understand that life, too. And in that way, none of us are outsiders.

CAROLINE LEAVITT is the *New York Times* bestselling author of thirteen novels, most recently *Days of Wonder*, which won praise from NPR, Zibby Media, the *Los Angeles Times*, the *New York Times*, the *Pittsburgh Post-Gazette*, *New Jersey Monthly*, *Boston Arts Fuse*, and more. It was also a CBS New York Book Club with Mary Calvi selection. Caroline is the recipient of fellowships from the New York Foundation for the Arts and from the Mid Atlantic Arts/New Jersey Individual Artist Foundation, as well as being a finalist for the Sundance Screenwriters Lab. Her work has appeared in the *New York Times*'s "Modern Love" column, *New York* magazine, the Daily Beast, and more. A book critic for *People* and for AARP's the *Ethel*, she is the cofounder of the book promotion platform A Mighty Blaze, and writes a column/blog for *Psychology Today*.

Brenda Janowitz

I Do It for Them (But Mostly for Me)

I did it every Friday. I would go to the charming little French bakery one town over and buy a big, delicious challah for Shabbat dinner. That night, we'd light candles, say prayers, and enjoy a family meal together. We did it because it was tradition; we did it because my son came home from elementary school one day and told me he was embarrassed to be Jewish. I wanted my children to understand where we came from.

Shabbat is the day of rest that begins on Friday at sunset and ends on Saturday after sunset, once three stars are visible in the night sky. Typically, Jewish families enjoy a festive Friday-night meal after the blessings are recited. For me, the centerpiece of this meal was, and has always been, the challah.

Friends said I should bake my own challah ("It's so easy!" they claimed), but I didn't have time. A busy working mom, I barely had time to *buy* the challah every week; I certainly didn't have hours to bake one from scratch.

But then, in March 2020, the world changed. On Friday, March 13, my sons didn't go to school and everything around me shut down. Quarantine began.

Suddenly, I had lots of time.

That first Friday in quarantine, I discovered that my cute little French bakery had temporarily closed. While I had chicken in the freezer that I could easily defrost for our Shabbat dinner, I wouldn't be able to buy challah, like I usually did, for Friday night. I fretted over what to do. I didn't want to lose the tradition of ringing in Shabbat with a challah, especially with the world feeling so uncertain. Everything seemed up in the air. When would the kids go back to school? When would I get back to work? What would be expected of my husband, who was a doctor during a world pandemic?

Tradition seemed more important than ever.

"Doesn't your friend Adrianne teach the kids how to bake challah?" my husband asked, and he was right. Adrianne came to our kids' Hebrew school once a year to lead the kids in a lesson on how to bake challah, and she also ran our synagogue's "Giant Challah Bake," leading temple members in a countrywide celebration.

I texted Adrianne and she immediately FaceTimed me.

"It's so easy!" she said, the refrain I'd heard so many times before. "Do you have a stand mixer?"

I did. I just hadn't used it, ever. I got it out and Adrianne guided me through the steps—instant yeast, butter, salt, sugar, eggs, and a touch of honey.

My friends were right—it's not difficult to make challah. It simply takes time. Patience. After putting together the dough, you knead it. Then you allow it to rise. Twice. Hours each time. Then you knead it again. One batch makes two loaves, symbolizing the double portion of manna collected on Fridays as the Jews wandered the desert upon their Exodus from Egypt. I made one traditional challah, and one with chocolate chips (which surely the Jews wandering the desert would have loved).

On Fridays during quarantine, instead of visiting that cute little French bakery one town over, I baked challah myself. I baked because I had no other option. I baked to maintain tradition. But also, an unexpected result: I baked because I enjoyed it. It felt so primal, making something with my hands for my family to eat. Something that generations of women had done before me. Kneading the dough, I felt at peace. I connected to women who also wanted a ritual to preserve who they were, and to remind their families of it.

Once quarantine was over, the little French bakery opened back up. Still, I found myself baking. *One more week,* I would tell myself. I told myself I was doing it for my kids, so that they'd understand where they came from, so that they'd understand the importance of tradition, but that wasn't it.

The truth was, I didn't want to stop. I was doing it for me.

As a working mom, my days are often a blur, starting from when my kids go off in the morning. I scramble to get my work done, and then, later, to be present for my kids, present for my husband, and then at the end of it all, I often collapse in my bed from exhaustion. Still, I can't sleep. The endless to-do lists run through my mind, even at 3 a.m. I trace the shadows on my bedroom wall as I tell myself that I'll get to everything tomorrow. I promise myself that I'll find time to get everything done.

But on Fridays, when I'm kneading the dough, my mind slows. As the to-do list anxiety builds, I tell myself that there's nothing to be done about it *then*, with my hands full of flour and dough. I couldn't do *that* errand right now, even if I wanted to. I couldn't answer *that* email until I was done kneading, until my hands were clean. I force myself to be present. I work the dough, pushing it back and forth, and think about this ancient ritual I'm taking part in, and what it means for my family. For me.

In the months since October 7, these meditative moments seem more important than ever. To remind myself why our traditions matter. To remind myself why we need to be proud of who we are. To remind myself how lucky I am to have my children come home to me at the end of the day, a luxury so many families no longer have.

An hour before dinner, I bake the challah I've made from scratch—the product of a full day's work—and then watch my husband and kids tear it apart. I'm left with a full tummy and an overwhelming sense of joy.

And the French toast that we make from leftovers on Saturday morning? Like manna from heaven itself, divine.

Brenda's Friend Adrianne's Challah Recipe

You'll need:

2 packages instant yeast
1 tsp. salt
One stick of butter or 6 Tbsp. canola oil, plus more to grease the bowl
Honey, to taste
5–6 Tbsp. sugar
4 eggs

4–6 cups flour, plus more for kneading
Chocolate chips (optional)

Preheat the oven to 350 degrees.

Combine both packages of instant yeast with 1¼ cups of warm water (approximately 110 degrees). Sit and let the mixture proof for about 10 minutes. It should become frothy.

Add the salt, then the butter, and mix either by hand or with a stand mixer.

Add honey and mix (eyeball the honey—I use a lot).

Add the sugar and mix. (Adrianne uses 5 Tbsp. I use 6 rounded Tbsp.!)

Add the eggs, one at a time, and mix.

Add the flour, one cup at a time, mixing until incorporated between the additions, at least 4 cups total. But you might need anywhere from 5–6 cups, depending on how sticky it is. Add more flour if needed.

Take the dough out of the mixer (or out of the bowl if mixing by hand), and, using more flour on the counter, knead it for 5 to 10 minutes. Then put it into a new greased bowl or pot to rise. Let it rise in a warm spot, covered, for an hour or two. The dough should double in size.

Once the dough has risen, I like to "punch" it down. Then take the dough out of the bowl/pot and knead it for another 5 to 10 minutes. Put the dough back into the bowl/pot and let it rise again, covered, for an hour or two. The dough should again double in size.

Take the dough out of the bowl/pot and knead it for another 5 to 10 minutes. You will have enough dough for two challahs. Divide into two sections. In each section, divide it further into three equal parts to then braid. I usually make one plain, and one with chocolate chips added in. (Add chocolate chips after all the flour is added but before you take it out of the mixer.)

Let the challah rise on a cutting board or platter, covered, for another half-hour.

Then make an egg wash (one egg, plus a little water) and brush it on the tops of both loaves. Bake the loaves on baking sheets at 350 degrees for 40 minutes.

BRENDA JANOWITZ is the author of eight novels, including *The Grace Kelly Dress*, which has been optioned for film by Hallmark Media, and *The Audrey Hepburn Estate*, which was chosen as the Readers' Choice by the CBS New York Book Club with Mary Calvi. Her work has also appeared in the *New York Times*, the *Washington Post*, *Real Simple*, the *Sunday Times* (London), *Salon*, *Redbook*, *USA Today*, *Bustle*, the *Forward*, the *New York Post*, *Publishers Weekly*, HelloGiggles, *Writer's Digest*, WritersDigest.com, and xoJane. She is the former books correspondent for PopSugar.

Samantha Greene Woodruff

Jew-"ish"

According to ancestry.com, my DNA is 98 percent Eastern European Jew. I have two Jewish parents. I had a bat mitzvah and can still recite my haftorah. But for most of my life I have been what my Protestant husband calls Jew-"ish."

One might call me a secular Jew, but I was less, even, than that. My Jewishness was a footnote to my identity as mother, wife, daughter, writer, yogi, brunette, short person with tall presence, aspiring rock star, Swiftie, therapy devotee, reluctant dog and reptile lover . . . The list goes on.

That changed after October 7, 2023.

Even then, it took me a while to publicly state that I was Jewish. I posted on social media that I was against terrorism and antisemitism, which meant I stood with Israel regardless of the current politics of the country itself. I liked other people's posts and shared them. But I never explicitly said that I was a Jew, nor acknowledged that it mattered.

The truth is, I've had a complex relationship with Judaism for most of my life. (Like any good Jew, I blame this on my mother.) My parents divorced when I was a toddler, and mom embraced her newfound independence, in part, by rejecting much of her strict Jewish upbringing. We didn't belong to a temple; we didn't even go for the high holidays. We did celebrate at home, dipping apples in honey on Rosh Hashanah, lighting candles for Hanukkah, and hosting a seder for Passover. But we also had a Christmas tree—*not* a Hanukkah bush. My dad, who'd never been religious, eventually remarried a lapsed Catholic. So, two Christmas trees.

I ended up going to Hebrew school and having a bat mitzvah to save my mom from my grandmother's relentless criticism of my lack of Jewish education. Apparently, it made her a bad mother. (Grandma Edith could be mean. She told me when I was six years old that I'd have no friends because my room was messy.)

I liked going to temple. I enjoyed feeling part of the community. I loved singing prayers and my haftorah (see above: aspiring rock star). I might even have blossomed into a practicing Jew had we not then studied "The Bible, as Literature" in my progressive private school. When I read the Passover story, it said "God hardens the Pharaoh's heart" so that Pharoah won't let the Jewish slaves go. This, in turn, enables God to inflict the ten plagues upon the Egyptians. *God wanted the ten plagues to happen?* I came home and told my mom: "God is a jerk." (I might have said something less innocent.) I then spent my teen and college years developing a strong antipathy toward organized religion.

In the husband-seeking years of dating, while my Jewish girlfriends sought Jewish men, I liked non-Jewish, nonreligious ones. No one was surprised when I married a non-practicing Presbyterian and went from Sam Greene to Samantha Woodruff. People only half joked that I was trying to pass as a WASP. Yes, I felt most at ease kibitzing with my Jewish friends, and my children's version of "oh, no" is "oy vey." But I also belonged to a country club that historically didn't admit Jews. And instead of standing up and saying, "Hello, I am Jewish," I, mostly, just tried to fit in.

Before we had kids, my husband and I decided that we would raise them "nothing." We were both basically atheists and I couldn't fathom them in Sunday school learning that Jesus is "the Christ," nor did I want them going to temple and being told they were the "chosen people." Still, it was important to me that my kids understood the Jewish part of their heritage. So, like my mother, I embraced Jewish traditions at home, in a secular way. But my big production holiday was and is Christmas. I start listening to carols on November 1. I have multiple trees, an ever-growing collection of nutcrackers, singing stuffed animals, and fancy glass ornaments. When they were young, my kids believed in Santa. (But not the Easter bunny. I didn't understand the bunny and told my kids that he probably didn't visit us because I was Jewish. I got them baskets and they knew it.)

I never hid my Judaism—I proudly kept Greene as my middle name—but I also didn't advertise it. After October, I convinced myself that if I was speaking out generally, it was enough. That was who I had always been. Privately, there was more to it. I was growing afraid. I didn't mind leaving some ambiguity around my Jewish identity, especially if it would protect my family.

And then things got scary. Jewish authors (and non-Jewish ones, too) who spoke out against the terrorist attack were appearing on viral blacklists. And I was one of them. The creators of these lists urged people not to buy our books, to unfollow us on social media, to tank our ratings with

one-star reviews. I was spared that, but many friends—
fabulous writers—were not.

And that's when I admitted to myself that I'd been hiding.
That's when I admitted I was scared. That's when my perspective on my Judaism changed. God and temple might not be my
thing, but I have an undeniable connection to Jewish people,
a comfort and ease that I don't feel elsewhere, and a shared
history of generational trauma that haunts me. The only way
I could manage the fear that, in our seemingly enlightened
world, our history is beginning to repeat was by circling up
with the people who get me at my very core. Religious or not,
my Jewish roots are deep. Judaism is in my soul. (For that, I
thank my mother—and, I guess, my grandmother, too.)

At this moment, when the rise of antisemitism in our world
is rampant, I see no choice but to boldly stand up against persecution, with my people. Whether or not I'm able to pass as
a WASP, I want to flaunt my Judaism like never before.

I'm no longer Jew-"ish." I'm JEWISH. But to be clear, this
doesn't mean I'm giving up Christmas.

SAMANTHA GREENE WOODRUFF has a B.A. in history from
Wesleyan University and an M.B.A. from the NYU Stern School
of Business. She spent nearly two decades working on the
business side of media, primarily at Viacom's Nickelodeon,
before leaving corporate life to become a full-time mom. In
her newfound "free" time, she took classes at the Writing
Institute at Sarah Lawrence College, where she accidentally
found her calling as a historical fiction author. Sam's debut
novel, *The Lobotomist's Wife*, was a #1 Amazon bestseller and
First Reads pick. Her writing has appeared in *Newsweek*,
Writer's Digest, Female First, Read 650, and more. Her second
novel, *The Trade Off*, will be released in Fall 2024.

Daphne Merkin

Passion and Pain

How can it be that less than a century after the worst genocide in history, when Jews were dragged out of closets to be sent off to be exterminated and babies were bashed against the wall, the curse of antisemitism has descended again? It is a question that many of my Jewish friends and I have been asking ourselves for months, ever since the Hamas incursion on October 7 unleashed a torrent of anti-Israel/antisemitic vitriol.

I don't recall feeling a sense of anxiety and panic about being Jewish as though it came with a stench all its own growing up, even though I was fully aware of the horrors of the Holocaust from an early age. I grew up in a Modern Orthodox family on the Upper East Side and went to a Jewish school. My parents were German Jews who had escaped Germany in the thirties because of the rise of Nazism. Unlike many survivors of the camps, however, who preferred not to talk about their experiences with their children, my mother was very open about the Holocaust and about the number of close relatives she had lost during those grim times. She bought two books that had been published for the Nazi press when she and my father went back to Germany that featured photos of Jews with their beards being cut off or being made to clean the streets with their hands.

Although there were times I felt self-conscious about my Jewishness, like when I walked down Park Avenue to synagogue on Yom Kippur wearing sneakers, I usually didn't. My three brothers didn't wear their yarmulkes outside the house until they were older. I mostly felt at ease with my identity and proud of the Jewish state. It would never have occurred to me to feel uncomfortable telling a cab driver that I was going to the Jewish Museum, like I did a few months ago. The truth is, I was afraid, for the first time in my life, to be marked as Jewish. That might seem paranoid: What *exactly* was I afraid of? I guess simply being the object of open hostility. It's a fear that continues to haunt me to this day.

My fear had spiked when, within ten days of the Hamas onslaught, the 2nd Ave Deli (which is actually on First Avenue and 75th Street) was defaced by a swastika that had been chalked or sprayed on its storefront. The restaurant, with its cozy diner décor, had always been a place of refuge for me, offering the Jewish (and kosher) equivalent of comfort food—chicken soup, gefilte fish, and chopped liver. The day after I went to the Jewish Museum, a small Jewish café on the Upper West Side, Effy's Café, was sprayed with red paint and antisemitic graffiti.

I think of words like "Jude" and "juif," of the inescapable marking of the yellow star, the stark hieroglyphic of the swastika, and the numbers burned into the arms of Jewish captives as though they were pieces of meat. I think of the appalling conditions of the ghettos, skeletal bodies piled up in the streets, and of the naked victims being shot in the back of the head and thrown into the pits—dug by Jews—at Babi Yar and other places. I think of Hitler's frantic speeches given at fever pitch, and the roaring approval of the crowds. I think, in short, that perhaps I have mistakenly taken something for granted, mistook a temporary reprieve for a new beginning and believed in "Never Again" as more than a slogan.

Jews, of course, have long been sensitized to the historical undertow of an implacable antisemitism that subsides only to reemerge at pivotal flashpoints, like eruptions in the Middle East or the latest kerfuffle in academia, which often trades in anti-Zionist rhetoric in the service of teaching the evils of structural inequity. Still, there have been years—decades, even—when overt antisemitism went mostly underground, especially in the wake of the Holocaust. After the establishment of the Jewish state, Israelis were seen as brave fighters instead of colonizers. Those days increasingly seem like a hallucination, or a pleasant delusion.

I am not sure what to make of Israel's current line of aggression toward the Gazans and other Palestinians and the destruction it has left in its wake—nor, I might add, do I know enough, no matter how much I read by military experts and seasoned political observers. But what I am sure of is that October 7 marked a lasting change in the country, a revival of a traumatic past. Israeli Intelligence, known for its ingenuity and infallibility, had failed, and Hamas had been sorely underrated.

Benjamin Netanyahu features very badly in all this, but I'm not persuaded that Israel wouldn't have had another devastating attack sooner or later if another leader had been in power. Israel's right to statehood was put in question from the day it was granted; not only has its sovereignty never been firmly established, but it has increasingly been treated as a pariah nation.

In the last year, I've been thinking a lot about my own move away from Jewish observance and the loss of that community, no matter how ambivalent my feelings were. Perhaps the constrictions served more of a purpose than I thought they had, ensuring a certain strength and resilience over a long and bloody history.

Over the decades I have frequently traveled to Israel, often taking my daughter with me, to shore up my sense of being part of a tribe. These days I feel lost, even unsafe, without an intact homeland to protect me. I don't trust some of my non-Jewish friends and have wondered whether any of them would take me in if the need arose. Perhaps being Jewish is to be permanently *other*, tolerated but not, when it comes down to it, accepted.

Jean-Paul Sartre, in his essay "Anti-Semite and Jew" (originally titled in French "Reflections on the Jewish Question"), published in 1946, posited that antisemitism was not merely a way of thinking, but a *passion*. Passions are not only impervious to logic, but have an unshakable grip on those they beset. The reflexive hatred of Jews is a tragedy we have been forced to withstand over and over again. It has weakened us but not destroyed us. My conviction is that whatever the cost, it never will. *Our* passion will never fade.

DAPHNE MERKIN is a critic, memoirist, and novelist.

Eleanor Reissa

A Hider

I was born and bred more than six decades ago in "the center of the universe," that great, diverse, inclusive city of New York. I lived there my whole life until COVID. In 2020, for the first time since I was born (in Brooklyn), I moved out of the city to a place that seemed safer, where I could live under the radar, with few streets, no subways, and not many humans.

My parents were Holocaust people: Jews who fought and lived through the Nazi, antisemitic, xenophobic horrors. Consequently, perhaps genetically, I have always kept one ear to the ground, listening for the sound of marching boots and peering into the distance for the shadows of smoke. That's how I am built. Perhaps too aware, too nervous, too fearful of history repetition. My fear primarily centers on injustice, that category that includes crimes of antisemitism, fascism, racism, homophobia, etc. There are so many.

I have been fearful all my life. Not just for myself, but for the identifiable others: the Jews, Muslims, trans and POC

who look the part, everyone who walks around with their yarmulkes or hijabs or hoodies or heels and makeup in full view
of those who hate them and would do them harm. I have
always worried for them—for the bearded Hasidic man out
and about on the streets or on the subway, with his tzitzit
hanging down, wearing his long woolen coat and hat in the
summertime. It's kind of silly, but I would try to sit near him
on the subway or stand next to him on the platform. For
support. Just in case. Maybe he'll need help (as though I can
help him). To comfort or ease him with a few Yiddish words.

"Hey, brider, ikh bin do. Kenst mit mir redn."

("Hey, brother, I'm here. You can talk to me.")

He and others live their lives openly and stand up to a
world where so many people want to erase them simply
because of their beliefs. Somehow they are not afraid. Or if
they are afraid, they carry on publicly anyway.

I have been a hider. Always. I never wear a Jewish star. I
changed my name to something Italian-sounding rather
than the Jewish name my father carried for all of his days. I
can "pass" and have done so for a lot of my life.

Then, October 7, 2023. What did that change for me?

It made everything worse. Heightened. My existential anxiety was not neurosis; it was reality. No need to imagine danger. It was real. I wanted to stand up and say, "I am here, you
haters. May you bring upon yourselves that which you wish for
us." But, of course, I would whisper this softly only to myself.

I also whispered to my brothers and sisters in the streets
and subways: "No, not a yarmulke today, brother! No, not
today. Someone will hurt you, someone will hit you, spit at
you. Please, brother, think about a Yankees or Mets baseball
cap."

But I don't say it. I have been mostly silent. This does not make me proud of myself.

This past April, I had to go to France. Whenever I fly I wear a particular fleece sweatshirt. One of my favorite things. It's warm and wooly and comforts me like a blanket. I took it down from the closet before I left for the airport. Then I realized that it had Yiddish writing on it. It says "der letzte valtz" in Yiddish letters, which means "the last waltz." It's from a klezmer music festival. Yiddish and Hebrew words are written with the same alphabet, so it all looks the same. Especially to a hater.

Also, I was going to bring along the book I was reading, *Bad Rabbi* by Eddie Portnoy. But I got nervous. Those items could identify me. Harm might come. I would be seen and known on the plane as "one of them." And so I brought neither the sweatshirt nor the book along. Hiding in full view.

I am sorry to be so afraid, especially since I am so far from the line of fire. However, the targets do keep moving, and what is "safe"? Soon it will be a year since the horror of October 7. I have done little to help, although I am in dialogue with people I don't agree with and do not run from that. The theater community that I belong to was mostly silent about the rapes and murders on that shabbat in October. There were some of us who tried to unite and connect with those on the other side, not very successfully, and as the war persisted, dialogue became nonexistent and hope for connection was lost. From what was supposed to be an empathetic community of artists, there was little comfort.

But I am my parents' daughter. My father was the only person from his transport to Auschwitz who returned to Stuttgart alive. Survival is nine-tenths of the law. Even though

I seem like a chicken, I will find my way to courage. I have become more articulate. And more visible. I seek to speak and engage nowadays, for whatever good that can do.

What also gives me hope is that Germany, that nation that committed so many crimes against the Jewish people and others a mere eighty years ago, is now an ally, a country that has tried to make amends.

As we approach the new year and the anniversary of this ongoing tragedy, may we have courage to stand up for who we are as humans and not bow to those who are hard-hearted and unjust.

ELEANOR REISSA is a multitalented artist: a Tony Award–nominated theater director, a Broadway and television actor, an international singer, and a writer. She has lived the life of storyteller in both English and Yiddish—her first language. She is a Brooklyn-born-and-bred victim/beneficiary of the New York City public school system. Her memoir *The Letters Project: A Daughter's Journey* sets out to discover the truth about her father, a slave in Auschwitz, as well as the truth about herself. The New York State Council on the Arts awarded her a grant to adapt her book into a play, and Eleanor received a nomination for Best Author Performance for an Audiobook by the SOVA Awards.

Her Broadway and television credits include Paula Vogel's *Indecent*, HBO's *The Plot Against America*, FX's *Dead City*, and most recently the German miniseries *The Zweiflers*, winner of best television series at the Cannes Film Festival 2024. Her recent films include *Musical Tales of the Venetian Jewish Ghetto* and *Noble Genius* with Hershey Felder. She is a prizewinning playwright, and her plays have been collected in an anthology, *The Last Survivor and Other Modern Jewish Plays*. She is the host of the Yale University/Fortunoff Video Archive podcast *Those Who Were There: Voices from the Holocaust*, now in its third season. From Carnegie Hall to international music festivals, Eleanor's powerful vocals have established her as a leading voice of Jewish song.

Jonathan Santlofer

Confessions of a Reluctant Jew

I am trying to remember the first time I knew I was Jewish. Perhaps I always knew. And didn't know. Didn't internalize it. Didn't get it. What it meant to be a Jew.

My parents were assimilated, "modern," nonobservant, so there was no *visible* religion. Working class and working hard to be American, my father from Queens, my mother from the Bronx, striving their way into the middle class and doing well. Because they traveled in exclusively Jewish circles (the only ones open to them at the time, something else I didn't know), it wasn't until they moved from "the city" to Long Island that I felt like an outsider.

It was the late 1950s. My sister and I were two of only three Jewish kids in our neighborhood. I was in third grade, nine years old, a small, sensitive boy. My first day of school I was bullied at recess, punched in the stomach by one boy while another two held me.

But what had I done? I had no idea. Until the next day when I heard the words hissed before the punch: "Jew Boy." I still didn't understand, but I guessed it was something bad, something to hide.

That Thursday night, like every Thursday night, we drove to the Bronx, where my grandparents hosted the family—my mother's five brothers, their wives and kids—raucous, fun-filled nights I remember as the happiest of my childhood. I used to joke that my mother's family was all light, and my father's all dark, though I didn't know why.

My mother's father, a natural storyteller, would gather the children and hold us enthralled with elaborately plotted tales of good guys and bad, gory comic-book violence, and heroic moral endings. (No surprise that when I later chose to write, it was crime fiction.) He was the kindest man I ever knew, and, though he was uneducated, the smartest. I adored him, confided in him, and vied to be his favorite.

I'd been afraid to tell my tough-boy-from-Queens father about the bullying, but once I was alone with my grandfather, I told him everything.

He listened and thought before he spoke.

"They do not know what they are doing," he finally said. "It is for you to teach them."

"But *how?*"

"You are a smart boy, kind, funny, and talented. Show them what you can do, draw them some pictures, make them laugh." He hugged me and told me it was the way we did things. When I asked him what he meant by *we*, he said, "Jews."

"But that's why they hit me, Grandpa!"

Lips pressed tight, he nodded slowly.

"Some people would say to hit them back, but what will that do? Only make them hit you harder. You need to show them *who you are*. I know, this is not easy. But remember, people are basically good."

He paused, then added, "Except for the *bad* ones!" and laughed, and I laughed, too.

I can't say this worked right away. There were a couple black eyes and bloody noses before they got bored because I wouldn't fight back. Meanwhile, I was making progress with the other kids, decorating looseleaf covers with cartoon characters, drawing "tattoos" with ballpoint pen on the toughest boys' arms. Soon I had friends. Even a girlfriend (my first), a WASPy blonde who lived on an estate with horses.

By the time I got to high school, Jews from Brooklyn and Queens had moved in (the Protestant kids fled, along with my girlfriend), and everything changed, even the geography. New housing developments (housing *communities*, my mother would correct me) were erected on what had been mostly farmland, with split-levels and ranch houses, landscaped and manicured, some with in-ground pools. (We had one, too, though no one in my family swam.) School became a hive of activity and ambition, all those college-bound Jewish kids whose parents dreamed of giving them a better life.

My mother took over as PTA president working hand in hand with the principal, an old-world white-haired Presbyterian. He admired her flair and chutzpah (a word he never would have known), and she, his calm counsel. While he taught her to consider the past, she got him to look at the future, and they became lifelong friends.

I was in graduate school when a friend of mine was collecting oral histories for the reopening of Ellis Island. I recommended she speak to my father's mother, whose circuitous tale of coming to America she often told, and I (thought) I knew. I will never forget listening to the tapes and hearing my friend ask, "So, Rebecca, what happened to the rest of your family?" and hearing my grandmother's answer.

"They died at Auschwitz."

I rewound the tape and listened again, then called my mother.

"Grandma didn't want to talk about it," she said, about her mother-in-law. "So we didn't."

I was twenty-one or twenty-two years old when I went to Ellis Island. Headphones on, I took the tour, listening to the mix of oral histories, and there, among them, was my father's mother, my grandmother, telling of leaving two babies and a husband behind in New York, of boarding a ship at the age of twenty-one or twenty-two herself, and going back to Poland to rescue her mother.

For the first time, I understood the darkness in my father's family. But I understood something else, something that had been passed down to me, a history and a culture. And it was then, at that moment, I felt and understood what it meant to be a Jew. I thought back to those elementary school bullies, and of my father's silent, often inflexible toughness, and of my grandfather, who I loved, and whose words still guide me.

"It is for you to teach them."

JONATHAN SANTLOFER is the author of the national best-selling novels *The Lost Van Gogh* and *The Last Mona Lisa*, the Nero Wolfe Award–winning *Anatomy of Fear*, the highly acclaimed memoir *The Widower's Notebook*, and six other novels, including the bestselling novel *The Death Artist*. He is editor and contributor of seven anthologies, including the *New York Times* notable book *It Occurs to Me That I Am America* and the bestselling serial novel *Inherit the Dead*. His short stories have appeared in the *Strand*, *Ellery Queen*, *Black Cat*, and numerous story collections. As an artist, Santlofer's work is in major private and public collections, including the Metropolitan Museum of Art, the Art Institute of Chicago, and Tokyo's Museum of Contemporary Art. He is the recipient of two National Endowment for the Arts grants, has been a visiting artist at the American Academy in Rome and the Vermont Studio Center, and serves on the board of Yaddo, the oldest arts community in the U.S. He lives in New York City, where he is at work on a new novel.

PART EIGHT

In Loving Memory

Rachelle Unreich

*To Cope with the Present, I Looked to My
Mother's Strength*

O n the first Sabbath after October 7, I went to synagogue. For most of my life, I had been an inconsis-
tent synagogue-goer, save for the period after my
mother, Mira, died, when I briefly became a regular visitor.
I could not exactly name what gave me comfort there, for
it felt like a whole mix of elements: the choral singing, the
uplifting renditions of the songs I had grown up with, the
familiar wooden seats, the dignified, impressive architec-
ture with its soaring domed ceiling, punctuated by a Star of
David at its center.

Grief had led me there then; after October 7, it made me
return. I yearned to be among others who would understand
how broken I felt, and how disoriented, in a world turned
upside down. I longed to hear my much-admired rabbi
deliver his usual elevating sermon, because he always made
sense of terrain that I could not navigate alone. It was only
when he stood up on the bimah that I realized how shatter-
ing recent events had been for everyone, including him. I was

expecting his usual eloquence, his brand of gentle wisdom, but the congregation and I received something entirely different. Hurt. Anger. Confusion. A week later, he apologized to those who had listened to his speech. On that day, words had failed him.

I'd always used words to climb my way out of troubling times. I was mired in sorrow for three years after my mother died, even though I knew this was not how I "should" feel—not when I ought to have been grateful. My mother had lived until three weeks shy of her ninetieth birthday. I had said my goodbyes; she had said hers. Throughout my life, she'd made me feel loved and whole. But her death splintered all that, and I was suddenly adrift. I tunneled my way out through writing, penning my mother's story of surviving the Holocaust, and all that she learned from it, in my memoir *A Brilliant Life.*

Ahead of its publication, I imagined a press tour in which I would tell colorful stories about my vibrant mother, Mira, and the fact that she had lived her life with so much joy, as well as strength. But it hit stores only weeks after October 7, and the landscape had changed completely since the book's inception. Suddenly I was hiring media training experts to prepare me for antagonistic questions, since I anticipated—correctly—that many journalists would ask me about the war in Israel. This, despite the fact that my book did not mention it, apart from when my mother visited her brothers there and decided she did not want to live there herself.

I wanted to fully enjoy every book launch and audience talk, but part of me was worrying about my daughter, whose Jewish school advised students not to wear their school uniforms on public transport, lest they find themselves a target for hate. One writers' festival hired a bodyguard for me, just in case. During my session at another festival, a protester stood up in the crowd, wearing a keffiyeh and holding a "Free Palestine" sign.

It was that protester who reminded me of the power of words once more. She stood up when a microphone was thrown to the audience for questions, presumably planning to be disruptive. Just before she did so, I started talking about how my mother, Mira, survived four concentration camps, including Auschwitz, and a death march at the age of seventeen. How both of her parents and two siblings were killed—her father shot before her eyes—and yet, when she gave testimony decades later, she said, "In the Holocaust, I learned about the goodness of people." How she focused on the people who helped her and saved her, Jewish and non-Jewish alike, rather than on those who tried to destroy her. How, if she were alive today, she would have preached the power of connection. How she chose to look at life with love, compassion, and kindness rather than with hate and resentment. While I said these things, the protestor put her sign down and walked away, her bluster defused.

I understood that it was not only my own writing that held force, but also my mother Mira's words, which I had faithfully recounted. It is not just what she endured that reaches readers' hearts, but who she was, and how she decided to live, despite everything. Her words and response to horror have given me a path to follow. Now, when I go to synagogue, I know it is to remember where I came from, and what attracted me to go there so often after Mira's death. It is the feeling I could never name, but I now know its source.

I never knew any of my four grandparents; all were brutally murdered in the Holocaust. They were born in the 1800s and had a completely different experience of life than my own. They often felt like historical figures. I would browse through their photos without a real understanding of who they were and how they lived. Yet if there is one aspect of my life that would be similar to theirs, it was going to synagogue. If they time-traveled to the present day, they would not feel out of place within its walls, which replicate the synagogues of Eastern Europe. They would recognize the tunes and know the Hebrew words of prayer. Going to synagogue reminds me on some deep, visceral level who I am, and what my ancestors held dearest.

It is something worth remembering now, more than ever. There's an irony about *A Brilliant Life* not lost on me: I've been promoting a book about antisemitism in a period where there's never been more antisemitism. I wrote it so that my mother's legacy would not be lost, but now I realize her lessons are more important and relevant than ever. Not just the lessons of history, and the dangers of it repeating. But my mother's template for how to live: with hope, resilience, and—perhaps most importantly—faith.

RACHELLE UNREICH is a journalist and author in Melbourne, Australia, and has written for newspapers and magazines including *Harper's Bazaar, Elle, Rolling Stone*, and the *Sydney Morning Herald* for the past thirty-eight years. Her first book, *A Brilliant Life: My Mother's Inspiring True Story of Surviving the Holocaust,* was published in the past year, appearing in ten countries, and has been shortlisted for several literary awards.

Barri Leiner Grant

Will All the Mourners Please Rise:
A Prayer for My Father

The margin of the photo is stamped *1945*. I sort through a small stash of pictures as we clean your home for the move to Memory Care. In this scalloped-edged black-and-white square, you are standing beside your dad. I know from the date that you are seven and that Grandpa Bernard will die of a heart complication just one year later. A faulty heart valve that could so easily have been replaced today.

I imagine my Grandpa Bernard Leiner, my namesake, is proud of you, his eldest. My Grandma Marge has likely snapped this keeper on the family Kodak Brownie.

When I was a kid, you told me that you regularly attended Park Synagogue with your family in Cleveland Heights. It was a conservative temple designed by the famous architect Erich Mendelsohn. An escapee from Nazi Germany, he was brought to Cleveland to design his first American synagogue commission. The centerpiece of the temple was a 125-foot hemispheric dome. You shared photos of its patinated copper exterior. As a bored kid, you'd try to count bricks during the long services while gazing up at that extraordinary ceiling. You also told me you stood to honor your father for a whole year following his death, reciting the Mourner's Kaddish.

When we joined Temple B'nai Israel in Rumson, I was in second grade. I recall your hand on my shoulder gently settling me back onto the bench when I rose by your side. You stood with all the other congregants who remembered the people they loved to recite Yizkor. I memorized the words with you and for you, this prayer of remembrance for which you stood up almost all your life.

It was 1995 when I moved my family from the East Coast to Chicago. I joined a conservative congregation of my own. I was deeply inspired by their young progressive rabbi, Elliott Cosgrove. He would lead sermons that began with things like, "This week in the *New Yorker*..." Current. Cool. I remember his rimless glass frames and the quiet kind of Clark Kent handsome he exuded. I felt proudly Jewish in a new way.

On the first high holy day of Yom Kippur, I rose with all who mourned to share prayer. This time for my mom. It was 1996, and she had been gone for three years. Rabbi Cosgrove read the prayer along with the others who stood for loved ones. The words were so potent and familiar; each breathed a knowing into my bones.

Yitgadal v'yitkadash sh'mei raba b'alma di-v'ra.

Rabbi Cosgrove asked us, in the kind of tone he'd use when imparting a lesson, "Do you know *why* we stand when we share this prayer?"

I always thought *you* stood up because you wanted to be closer to your dad in heaven. Later still, I thought you stood up so that your head would be close to G-d in reverence. The rabbi told us, "It is so that the community can see who is hurting, who needs our help and hand while grieving." The prayer itself honors G-d and does not say anything directly about grief, grieving, or the bereaved. I admired his explanation.

You've lost most of your memories. Now I mourn the loss of untold stories. I write down those I know. I tell them to my girls. I memorize your hands. Your eyes. Brown. Your favorite color. The kind of brown that matched your old Chrysler Cordoba, the one with Corinthian leather seats, an 8-track player, and a CB radio you installed.

"Breaker one-nine for a radio check."

You'd let us play along with the truckers. It felt so grown-up. Your new company car, just one of many of your ad agency perks. Our brilliant Ad Dad.

You were famous for creating winning headlines, product names, and even Breast Cancer Awareness Day. Now you struggle just to recall the appropriate word. Some days, the words land like my old gymnastics vaults: executed with pride and a shaky landing. I consider some of your words to be a language *we* speak, one that is all our own. I guess at the words in rapid-fire bursts, like we are on a new game show with the clock ticking. I let others go and we enjoy a belly laugh together when we just can't get it right.

I realize, too late, that I am experiencing our lasts. We listen to music known and loved, like the songs of Ray Charles. You used to sing along, and tap a foot, but no more. I recite kaddish and search for a glimmer. Gosh, I long for a glimmer.

A friend shared that her entire congregation is rising for kaddish, so no one is left standing alone. I know how much you would like that. I told you.

Dad, may the whole wide world stand for all who grieve and know the deep loss of dementia. May I keep your memories alive, always.

Amen.

BARRI LEINER GRANT is a well-respected grief specialist, author, founder, and Chief Grief Officer® of The Memory Circle: for those learning to live with loss. As coach, educator, and advocate, she holds transformative gatherings and workshops to explore grief-tending tools and techniques that foster community, hope, and healing.

Her work has been featured in the *Washington Post, Psychology Today,* and Maria Shriver's the *Sunday Paper,* among others. Her mother, Ellen, died suddenly in 1993. Her dad, Neil, lives with dementia. She honors them in this work. She lives with her two children, Emma and Quinn; her husband, Alex; and their pup, Bean, in New York.

Annabelle Gurwitch

Shalom, Y'all

Between 1887 and the start of World War II, more than 2 million Eastern European Jews landed on America's shores. Many arrived at Ellis Island, looking like a bus and truck touring company from *Fiddler on the Roof,* with only the clothes on their backs and a letter vouching for them from a family member who'd already immigrated. There were wealthy Austro-Hungarian Jews immigrating, but those weren't my people. One of my ancestors was a peddler. He traveled from shtetl to shtetl, selling junk off the back of a swayback mule. A friend who was descended from landed gentry once asked if we Gurwitches had a family crest.

"Why, of course!" I answered. "It has a mule, a potato, and the gunnysack where we stash our enormous wealth and space lasers."

The majority of Jews settled in the big northern cities like New York and Philadelphia, while others entered the country through Boston or southern ports like Charleston.

My great-grandfather Bert Gurwitch and his family left
Russia, fleeing the pogroms and seeking to better their lot
in life. By trade, Bert was a shipyard welder, so the family
followed the shipbuilding work in coastal cities, starting in
Quincy, Massachusetts, then headed south to Charleston,
farther south to Chickasaw, Alabama, and finally settling
in Mobile, where they joined other Russian immigrants,
including my grandmother's family. The Jewish population
of Mobile has never been greater than it was in 1918, with
more than 2,200 Jews.

My grandmother Rebecca always stressed the importance
of knowing who someone's "people" were. She never took into
account that people might not like us if they considered who
our people were. Malcolm Gladwell wrote in the *New Yorker*
in 2014 about "climbing the crooked ladder of success," as
a way of describing how immigrant families worked on the
margins to become respectable pillars of society. Their aim
wasn't the establishment of a criminal empire, it was the
advancement of the clan.

Bert found his welding skills to be invaluable in maintain-
ing local bootleggers' stills, and that's how he wound up in
the white-lightning moonshine business. Bert's wife, Rose,
my great-grandmother, was an enterprising balabusta. The
family had opened a dry-goods store by then and customers
knew to tap a sterling-silver cup, probably a kiddush cup, on
the counter. For ten cents, Rose would pour you a swig of
moonshine from the pickle barrel. Same cup for everyone.

My cousins have made me take a blood oath not to write
that Rose was in a league with sex workers, but she did rent
out rooms behind the store to a cadre of hardworking women
with ladders of their own to climb. What no one in the family
disputes is that during the 1950s, when Rose's tenant Edna

answered the door, you'd say, "The Gurwitches sent me," and she'd show you right in. That's right: The only door being a member of my family ever opened led to a brothel.

By the time I entered the picture, Rose was a kindly elder, five feet at most, who wore blousy housedresses, clunky ortho-pedic shoes, and Coke-bottle wire-rimmed glasses. She spoke only Yiddish, but kissed and pinched our cheeks, delighted in watching her great-grandchildren play, and rewarded us with hard candies from a cut-glass bowl in the living room of her modest home.

In those early years, Mobile was segregated by race, eth-nicity, and religious affiliation. As a teenager, my father and his cousins would sneak out on Saturday nights. The Klan met just before midnight in a local clearing. The boys would peek from the relative safety of the surrounding trees as they watched with horror as the Klan spewed their hate-filled rhetoric around a bonfire.

Private clubs wouldn't accept Jews, so Jewish Mobilians formed the Ladies Aid Society and the men founded the Jewish Progressive Club. These groups provided relief from the restricted social scene by hosting a variety of entertain-ment, along with sponsoring charitable projects dedicated to uplifting the community.

The Jews in Mobile intermarried, founded houses of wor-ship (fill in that well-worn joke about two Jews/three syna-gogues), and did business together. They pooled resources to ensure that all of my father's generation, the first born on American soil, could be sent to college. This banding together, as my cousin Neal has reminded me, wasn't neces-sarily out of affection, it was out of necessity.

Things didn't change that quickly. When my cousin Robin tried to join her high school classmates in becoming a debutante, she was denied. Mobile didn't see its first Jewish deb until 2015.

In the Ahavas Chesed synagogue's oneg shabbat room, a framed tablecloth is displayed on the wall. The cloth was painstakingly hand-embroidered with Jewish stars by the Ladies Aid Society in 1952. Stitched alongside each angle of each star are the names of members of the congregation. I'm related to all of them. It's like a Gurwitch Shroud of Turin. Proof of the intertwined and imaginative invention of the Shalom, Y'all tribe, not an assimilation, but a singular mash-up of old world, Gulf Coast traditions.

How did they metabolize the shvitzing shock of the humidity, the sandy soil, the scrubby pines? Rose kept a kosher home, so how did she square the prohibition to shellfish with the low country lousy with temptation? "God forgive me," Rose, ever adaptive, repeated each time she ate an oyster, which was very often, earning her a reputation as the most deeply prayerful brothel owner in Mobile.

My father longed for the larger world, which is how I wound up being raised in Miami Beach, where for many years my connections to the immigrant experience took the form of reenacting Rose's ritual and playing Fruma-Sarah, a vengeful, enraged ghost, in the Temple Beth Sholom production of *Fiddler*. I chalk up the fact that I'm not a shut-in to the fortuitousness of the absence of footage of what I'm certain was a terrifying portrayal. Not terrifying in the way one might expect of an angry specter, but terrifying in the way that a preteen portraying an aggrieved dead widow can go off the rails.

Most in my generation who were born in Mobile have ventured far and wide, at least physically. I have followed the family tradition of coastal living, but as a noncongregational atheist, I belong to a gaggle of artist tribes. As my friend and colleague Lisa Hostein, executive editor of *Hadassah*, puts it, "There are many ways to do Jewish." I revel in boho-inspired multicultural meldings like Seder over the Rainbow, presided over by a cantor in a Cowardly Lion costume, or a silent disco Tashlich on the banks of the Los Angeles River. And, as the drumbeat of anti-immigrant sentiment has risen, so has my commitment to extending a Shalom, Y'all welcome to those fleeing twenty-first-century pogroms.

We welcome the stranger for we were once strangers in the land of Egypt. I welcome the stranger for we were once strangers in Bayou La Batre.

This is why I said yes without hesitation when my dear friend and Broadway star Jessica Hecht recruited me to lead writing workshops with the Campfire Project. It was portraying Golde in the 2016 Broadway *Fiddler* revival, staged to evoke the unfolding humanitarian crisis as tens of thousands of Syrians seeking asylum turned up on Greek shores, that stirred Jessica's immigrant roots. Channeling the strength of all the Goldes that ever were, Jessica set out to provide relief in the form of arts education by connecting the theater community, another tribe I claim membership in, with young asylum-seekers from Anatevkas around the globe. Since 2018, Campfire has brought what Jessica calls "a carnival for the body and soul" to resettlements and refugee camps in Ritsona, Greece, Moldova, and Uganda.

In July of 2024, Campfire set up shop at the Midtown Manhattan headquarters of the Workers Circle, originally known as Der Arbeter Ring, founded by garment workers in 1892 to promote Jewish cultural engagement and social justice activism. Jessica's grandmother Rose was a lifelong activist.

For one week, the Campfire team of artists and educators, ladder climbers all, wrote, sang, danced, created theater and art, and shared meals with young asylum-seekers from countries including Guinea, China, and Ecuador. We witnessed these youth stretch themselves into their own singular cultural mash-ups. A ten-year-old described a delicious-sounding Kabuli Pulao, an Afghan lamb-and-rice dish, while enthusiastically tasting Mexican food for the first time.

"I am so Venezuela, coasts and mountains, and you are so New York, streets and buildings," Helkiss, a teenage Venezuelan, waxed poetic in the writing workshop.

My bones are made of gumbo, stuffed cabbage, knishes, and 100 percent humidity, not asphalt and glass, but I didn't correct Helkiss. I was too busy marveling at the making of this extraordinary new American and wondering what great-grandma Rose would make of him, who I consider a member of our Shalom, Y'all tribe. I tend toward the sentimental, a luxury afforded to the second generation, but Rose was practical above all. She'd probably have tried to sell him her white-lightning moonshine.

ANNABELLE GURWITCH is a *New York Times* bestselling author of five books, including her most recent essay collection, *You're Leaving When?* Her work appears in the *New Yorker*, the *New York Times*, the *Washington Post*, and *Hadassah Magazine*, among other publications. She is honored to be a featured artist alongside Tony Kushner and Alfred Uhry at the Museum of the Southern Jewish Experience in New Orleans. She is a two-time finalist for the Thurber Prize for American Humor.

Courtney Sheinmel

Connection

My son, Archer, was not even a year and a half old when the oncologist told us that there weren't any treatment options left for his Grandma Elaine. It was the second summer of COVID, and hospital regulations dictated that only one family member visit at a time. But that day, my mom had special permission to have three of us there with her, because of the gravity of the news being delivered.

"I won't be at Archer's bar mitzvah!" she had sobbed. The memory of those words in her voice is marked on my heart like the thick scar of a burn.

Someone gave my stepdad a phone number to set up home hospice care. For a month, he, my sister, and I orbited around my mom, our sun, as her light dimmed and dimmed and dimmed. I was holding one of her hands when she took her last breath.

Rosh Hashanah came a few weeks later. I hadn't been to high holiday services since I was a kid. But I remembered well the words the rabbi said each year:

On Rosh Hashanah it is written, on Yom Kippur it is sealed
Who shall live and who shall die

Was God real? Had he really planned for my mom to die when she did?

My mother had known her diagnosis. But she had planned for life. After her death, I found a list she'd made just a couple months earlier. There in her lovely script were the names of all the people she'd planned to invite for a holiday meal.

My stepdad, my sister, and I talked about what to do. The fall of 2021 wasn't exactly lockdown anymore, though things were still dicey. Plus we were deep in fresh grief, and none of us felt up to playing host to a meal without my mom. We barely even knew the prayers. I mean, we knew them. But not like my mom did.

We decided to be together as a family but not invite anyone else. *Sorry, Mommy,* I said to her in my head, as I looked around her dining room table with empty chairs. In the old days, there wasn't a seat to spare. She'd add card tables as extensions and borrow more chairs from the neighbors.

The old days felt like the *real* days. It felt like any day now, my mom would come back, and real life would resume.

But, of course, that's not how it works. Death is forever, and the lives of the people my mother loved best kept on going without her. My sister adopted a new dog. My stepdad bought new glasses. My son went from speech-delayed to chatterbox.

I spent a lot of time contemplating what happens after you die. Was it like a candle snuffed out, or was there something more—an afterlife, perhaps? Could my mother see us? Did she feel our enduring love, and love us back? Did she miss us? When it came to the latter, I genuinely hoped not. Missing was so painful. Her death has caused us that pain; but I hoped it spared her.

I talked to her constantly, a running narrative in my head. One night, Archer and I both had a stomach bug. I slept in his room, feeling terribly ill and terribly alone. I ached to connect with my mother.

"Mom," I said out loud, softly, so as not to wake Archer. "Where are you?"

QUACK! QUACK! QUACK!

A baby toy of Archer's went off at full volume. It was a duck (obviously) that quacked when you squeezed its middle. It had never spontaneously quacked before. I leapt up, grabbed it, and muffled it under my pillow. The quacking stopped.

Then something occurred to me. I pulled out the duck and regarded it. This little toy, about the size of my hand. Its yellow feathers taking on a bluish hue in the dark.

"Mom, are you here?"

QUACK! QUACK! QUACK!

"Oh my God."

The toy wasn't from my mom. I didn't remember her having any connection to ducks when she was alive. I googled the next morning and read that birds are seen as messengers of God in Judaism. They're believed to be able to connect the spiritual world to the physical one.

Had that just happened to us in the middle of the night in my toddler's bedroom? It seemed like wishful thinking. But yellow ducks kept popping up. I saw them on business logos, people's socks, and decals in the pediatric ER, where my son went for an infected bug bite. One day I was walking on an empty stretch of beach with one of my mom's dearest friends. Archer ran ahead of us to grab something he'd spotted in the sand: a yellow rubber duck.

I knew it could be a coincidence. I knew it was likely there'd always been duck socks and duck decals around me, and I was only noticing them now. But I decided to believe that all those ducks were signs that even as time marched forward, my mother was still with us, in her way.

We continue to do our best to keep her close. Photos of her adorn my apartment walls. Our family talks about her every day. The day after the second anniversary of her death, my octogenarian stepdad and I got matching tattoos inspired by my mom's maiden name. And we started inviting friends over for the Jewish holidays again, just as she would've done, though we breezed through prayers faster than she ever did—in part because we didn't know them as well, and in part because it remained hard to say them without her.

Sometimes I'd run through the list of things my mom was missing. Every day, the list grew longer, and time was doing that weird twisty thing it does, making it hard to remember if certain things had happened before she'd died, or after.

Two years, two months, and one week after my mom died, it was October 7, 2023. There was a surprise attack by a terrorist group. Hamas slaughtered more than a thousand civilians in Israel and took more than two hundred forty additional hostages back to Gaza. It was the largest attack on the Jews since the Holocaust—something my Grandma Diane, my mother's mother, had escaped, while every other member of her family was murdered.

"I'm glad Mommy wasn't here to see," my sister and I said to each other, which was simultaneously absolutely true and absolutely untrue. The Jewish high holidays had just passed. I remembered those haunting words:

On Rosh Hashanah it is written, on Yom Kippur it is sealed
Who shall live and who shall die

A week later, I told my son we were going to light the candles for Shabbat. It was something I'd never done with him before. But I imagined hundreds of families in Israel, missing their loved ones, lighting candles, crying desperate prayers. I wanted to add our prayers to the chorus. I had candlesticks from my mom. I paused Archer's post-dinner YouTube video and he stood beside me as I stumbled through the prayer that I knew my mom would've known better. If only she were with us.

But the next week, I knew it better, too. The third Friday we said the Shabbat blessing, I struck the match to light the candles, and my son's little voice began:

Baruch ata Adonai . . .

He shocked me by reciting the whole thing. It was beautiful. It was magical. It was ineffably sad. My heart squeezed from the urge I always have in such moments to send a text to my mother and tell her about it.

Archer and I watched the candles burn for a minute or two. Then he wanted to go back to his YouTube video, which I'd set on pause. We walked over to the TV, I picked up the remote, and as I pointed it, I noticed what was frozen on the screen: a bunch of barn animals . . . including a bright yellow duck.

"Mom?" I whispered. "Are you here?"

Loss doesn't happen simply on the day your loved one dies. It repeats at every milestone, every holiday, every world event, every ordinary moment, and even every prayer. It's impossible to feel my mother's presence now without also feeling her absence. Sometimes it seems as if I only dreamed her. It helps to connect to something bigger, like those Friday nights that I stand next to my son to light candles and recite a prayer.

Archer, only four years old, was oblivious to it all. He happily settled back down in front of the TV, leaving me to ponder all the unanswerable questions:

Was my mom with us somehow? Did she hear her beloved grandson recite the prayer? Can she feel our unending love? Does she know the secrets of the universe—or at least when the hostages might come home? Who shall live and who shall die?

And, Mom, what is up with all those ducks?

COURTNEY SHEINMEL is the author of nearly thirty books for kids and teens, including the acclaimed *Stella Batts* and *My Pet Slime* series for young readers. Her book *Helen Keller* was part of Chelsea Clinton's She Persisted series.

Jennifer S. Brown
Mourning Rituals

Someone needed to write letters to the recently bereaved for my synagogue. The previous volunteer was retiring, moving across the country. The letters weren't sympathy notes but instructions on the Jewish traditions of mourning, the calculations of the dates of remembrance, and a way to let the mourner know that they weren't alone at such a vulnerable time.

No one wanted the job—and I understood why. The Jewish calendar can be a beast, a lunar calendar that shifts from year to year, plus there are seven leap months in a nineteen-year period, which means an entire extra month of sliding dates backward. Shiva is a seven-day mourning period, but it can't end on Shabbat. *Shloshim* is a thirty-day mourning period, but holidays can cancel or delay both shiva and *shloshim*. If a death occurs after sundown on, say, a Thursday, then the secular day of death is Thursday, but the Hebrew date of death is Friday. Mourning laws are different for parents, as opposed to spouses or siblings. Making a mistake in the calculations is all too easy—and what could be more horrific than making a mistake about honoring a loved one?

No wonder no one wanted to do it.

But it's an important job, a necessary job. And a volunteer was needed.

"Why don't *you* do it?" a friend on the bereavement committee suggested, with a note of pleading in her voice.

At the time, my children were seven and five years old and my time to volunteer at the synagogue was limited. Most of my waking hours were spent raising my kids. But *maybe* I could write letters at home in the evenings when they were in bed.

"I could do it for a few years," I said.

That was fourteen years ago.

I'm a descendent of a long line of Jewish socialists— politically active atheists who took great pride in their Jewish heritage but who observed minimally. They felt strongly that the Jewish community was to be supported and nurtured. Like them, I find there is much about traditional Judaism that doesn't make sense. Why can't I eat pork? Why is a menstruating woman unclean? Why should the interpretation of text tell me who I can love?

But one thing I've always admired is the Judaic mourning rituals. I've attended the wakes, funeral masses, and celebrations of life of many cultures and appreciated how they provide comfort for those who have experienced a loss. Yet, in most cases, that's where it ended. After the burial or ceremony, the mourner returned to a life of the living. *Time to put grief aside and move on.*

In Judaism, mourning *begins* with the burial. Mourners return from the cemetery, and shiva begins. Mirrors in the house are covered, so we don't witness our grief. We sit on stools close to the ground to symbolize how death has brought us low. Doors are left unlocked so people can enter to express their sympathy without distracting the mourners, without forcing them to play host. For the seven days of sitting shiva, the community comes out to mourn, bringing food and comfort. Tradition holds that you don't speak to the mourner until they speak to you; some people want to talk about the deceased, while others prefer to sit in silence with their thoughts.

Mourning is personal and is to be respected.

But shiva doesn't end the mourning, either. Next is *shloshim*, the thirty days after burial, when the mourner reenters the world but is still grieving. Every day, the Mourner's Kaddish is recited—in more traditional communities, three times a day—with a minyan, a quorum, of ten Jewish people, because one shouldn't grieve alone.

The unveiling occurs after eleven months, minus one day, when the gravestone is uncovered at the cemetery.

Finally, mourning ends after twelve months. But that doesn't mean the person is forgotten; every year, on the anniversary of the death, the Mourner's Kaddish is recited among a minyan.

Writing bereavement letters can be depressing, especially when the deceased or the bereaved is a friend. Yet I never feel as much a part of my Jewish community as I do when sending those letters. Each calculation of dates ties me closer to my people. Explaining when rituals are performed helps the mourner on their journey through grief. Writing letters is an act of caring, of reaffirming my beliefs. Helping others through difficult times is one of the most Jewish acts a person can perform.

Our mourning rituals demonstrate Judaism's value of caring for one another. With our traditions, we keep the deceased alive in our hearts. As we say, "May their memory be a blessing for you."

So many things about Judaism confuse me, but not this. In doing this act of service, I've become an integral part of my community, just as my own ancestors were. The legacy of generations past continues.

JENNIFER S. BROWN is the author of the historical novels *The Whisper Sister* and *Modern Girls*. She holds a B.F.A. in film from NYU and an M.F.A. in creative writing from the University of Washington. She lives outside Boston with her family.

Danny Grossman

Once and Again

The tiny train station was drab and creepy, and it only got worse when I wandered out of its rickety front door. Yep, Starokonstantinov, the place my ancestors called home one hundred years ago, was mostly made up of low-slung, uninspired buildings, each one the same bleached-out color of dirty sand. What had once been a Ukrainian shtetl, precariously positioned between Berlin and Moscow, was nearly obliterated during World War II. No maps, no street signs, no nothing—I was officially lost.

Walking along, I noticed a significant military presence, and I couldn't help but wonder how a U.S. diplomat (that would be me) serving in the Soviet Union (that would be Leningrad) during the Cold War (that would be 1985) ever got permission to visit this godforsaken area. But there I was, a twenty-six-year-old Foreign Service officer, trudging through the village of my roots, in search of some sort of . . . well, I wasn't exactly sure what I was looking to find. Maybe a good story for my dad back in San Francisco, maybe a link to my past, or maybe just some scrap of hope I could carry into the future.

I tried approaching locals for directions to the historic spots, but every time I explained that I really wanted to see the cemetery, particularly the prewar one, all responded with the same go-away glare and terse answer: "The old buildings were destroyed. There is no cemetery." At last, one elderly woman took pity. "There might be something on the outskirts," she mumbled, without pausing for eye contact.

Two miles down a bumpy road, and a few wrong turns later, I reached the graveyard, made my way to the Jewish section, and began scanning tombstones for familiar names. Grossman? Kaufman? Perlmutter? The closest one I came across was Groysman, the Yiddish version of Grossman, but nothing tracked to my genealogical research. Still, I knew that this was the town where my people lived, and where they died.

Indeed, Starokonstnatinov's Jewish population, including many of my relatives, were slaughtered, both by ordinary Ukrainians who became lawless thugs hungry to scapegoat their neighbors and German soldiers "just doing their job."

Had this town once been teeming with blacksmiths and butchers, schools and synagogues, shops and gardens, kids playing, friends chatting, tender mercies and wild beauty and genuine possibility? Was there laughter here? Music? Books? Wisdom? Joy? Was Starokonstantinov—now filled with ghosts—once filled with love?

Just beyond the new Jewish cemetery, I finally found the prewar one. It was set on a cliff above the town and it had very obviously been violated. Tombstones were in pieces. Hebrew words inscribed on their fragments were scattered across the field. Had this space been desecrated before the war or was it savaged after? Had human beings become so adept at dehumanizing their enemies that even the dead were not spared? I had no way of knowing when it happened. I only knew that for a time in Starokonstantinov, to be a Jew was to be blamed for whatever was wrong in the world.

I stood for a while. I walked for a while. I wept for a while. I couldn't find my kin, but I could feel their presence, as sure as I could feel my heartbeat. My great-aunt Polina's sisters, their husbands, and their babies—the ones who were shot at Babi Yar or starved or trampled or beaten to death in yet another horrific pogrom—were standing and walking and weeping beside me in this once sacred place, now shattered by hate.

If October 7 proved nothing else, it proved that a pogrom, intended to ravage the spirit and crush the soul, is all too easily resurrected. But the Hamas attack was carried out in the State of Israel, not Starokonstantinov, and Israel is a community of astonishing resilience. It is a ray of light for Jews living in an increasingly dark universe, much the same way that, despite everything, the U.S. is still the promised land for any number of migrants around the globe.

Either by coincidence or fate, only two days after the terrorist assault, I was standing, along with eight other members of my synagogue, in the baggage claim of San Francisco International Airport, waiting to welcome a refugee family from Ukraine. Kolya and Natasha Taranov, along with their daughters, nine-year-old Nikol and her twelve-year-old sister, Nelli, were fleeing Russian aggression from the same country so many in my family were unable to flee all those years ago. About the only thing I knew of the Taranovs was that they were going to arrive with frayed nerves and two pet cats.

Actually, I knew one other thing: These people needed my help and, given how totally powerless I was feeling at that moment in time, I desperately needed to be helpful.

There were schools to register for, job applications to fill out, driverless cars to explain, English words to decipher, sights to see. And so it was that on a fog-free Sunday afternoon, we walked across the Golden Gate Bridge, from San Francisco to Marin County. Along the way, they saw sea lions splashing across the Pacific Ocean, Angel Island, and Point Bonita Lighthouse. They saw the mountains touch the sky.

And what I saw was a link to my past, a story I wish I could tell my dad, and a scrap of hope I could carry into the future.

DANNY GROSSMAN served in the U.S. Foreign Service as a diplomat overseas and at the Department of State, with a focus on human rights. He went on to become the CEO of the San Francisco Bay Area Jewish Community Federation and Endowment Fund. Previously, he founded Wild Planet Entertainment, where he was CEO for eighteen years. Danny; his wife, Linda Gerard; and their two sons, Noah and Jonah, currently reside in Northern California.

PART NINE

Happy(?) Holidays

Lisa Kogan

What Are You Doing New Year's Eve?

It's been a long time since I've believed in God, though I worry that this God I don't believe in will be mad at me and I'll end up with an asymmetrical bob or a bad credit score.

Still, I like Rosh Hashanah. I like putting out cloth napkins and supermarket flowers and my mother's wedding china. I like pomegranates and dates and the way our neighbors always show up with the really good challah from that Hungarian bakery on Second Avenue. I like how our dog discreetly positions himself directly under the toddler at the table for any fallen-brisket opportunity that might present itself. I like watching my husband guilt people into putting their phones away. I like hearing my pal, Judith, announce that she just wants to live long enough to see her grandchildren pick a gender. I like getting out a yellow legal pad, writing down the crummiest thing that happened to each of us since we last gathered, then ripping our long list of sorrows into confetti. I like everyone grabbing a handful of the confetti and tossing it into the air just before we dip slices of Granny Smith apples into farmer's market honey. I like leaning in and catching up and wondering where the time goes.

Has it really been almost 365 days since Hamas carried out the deadliest attack on Jews since the Holocaust? Have four entire seasons come and gone since I watched college campuses explode in rage, since I crossed the street to avoid a guy shouting antisemitic slurs in front of my corner bodega, since I first wept for Palestinian civilians and despaired for tortured hostages and watched the world go off its rocker?

I hold my annual savory versus sweet kugel debate, just as my mother used to do. What would she have made of all this darkness? I open the box that holds her old recipes on stained index cards and trace her loopy handwriting with my fingertip. My mom would not have crossed the street. I clean carrots, smash garlic, and chop onions. My mom guided Detroit schoolkids through the Holocaust Memorial Center. I dust, I vacuum, I tell myself I'd be doing this even if we didn't have company coming. My mom knew how to talk and she knew how to listen and she knew that some people have been through the kind of pain that can harden a heart. I order red wine and add an extra leaf to the dining table. My mom did not suffer fools, but she also understood that a rose is not its thorns—she had a way of answering fear with fact, cruelty with compassion. I call the liquor store back and ask for three more bottles of cabernet. It's been that kind of year.

The doorbell will start ringing at around 7 p.m. We are— the vegan duck incident of 2019 notwithstanding—a pretty mellow group. We run the gamut from two to ninety-six years of age. We've got Buddhists, Catholics, Jews, and your occasional lapsed Protestant. We come in a variety of colors, orientations, and income levels. I guess our common bond is that every single one of us is more than ready to say goodbye to the year 5784 on the Jewish calendar. So, at sundown, we'll light the candles and we'll recite the prayers. I'll look around the table and remember when my daughter was little and my mom was here. Once dinner is done, some of us will curl up on the sofa and talk late into the night and some of us will hang out in the kitchen, transferring food from big Tupperware containers into slightly smaller Tupperware containers. All of us will be taking stock of our lives and missing somebody we love and thinking about the future.

It never occurred to me last Rosh Hashanah that Israel would be at war on this Rosh Hashanah, nor did I understand that this war could unleash a fury that would ricochet around the globe. But here we are, all of us weary, all of us anxious, all of us looking for something we can believe in, all of us hoping for better days ahead.

LISA KOGAN is the author of *Someone Will Be with You Shortly: Notes from a Perfectly Imperfect Life,* the ghostwriter of several *New York Times* bestselling books, and an acclaimed speech writer. She was an award-winning columnist at *Elle* and was *O, The Oprah Magazine*'s writer-at-large for twenty years.

Renée Rosen
Remembering Kristallnacht

I'm not what anyone would consider an observant Jew—
I've always been more spiritual than religious. But I did
grow up in a Jewish home, and our conversations were
always peppered with Yiddish phrases. My grandfather left
Warsaw in the early 1900s and established himself as a musi-
cian and photographer in the States. He and my grandmother joined us every Sunday morning for smoked fish,
lox, and bagels from the only Jewish deli in Akron, Ohio.
We went to services on the high holidays and cultivated our
own holiday traditions. I remember our abbreviated Passover seders with a Maxwell House Haggadah stained with
red horseradish from years gone by. I reluctantly attended
Hebrew school and was bat mitzvahed. But memorizing my
haftorah portion from a tape recording without ever knowing what any of it meant left me feeling empty.

I've always maintained that Judaism isn't something I can
express in specific prayers and rituals, which hold little meaning to me—it's something I carry in my heart. Growing up,

I had questions about my religion and was troubled by the fact that we, as a people, are ambiguous about whether or not we believe in an afterlife. All this and more set me on a spiritual journey.

As I grew older, I began to study the teachings of Nichiren Shōshū Buddhism. I chanted twice a day and recited chapters of the Lotus Sutra in Sanskrit. In my eyes, none of this negated the fact that I was still Jewish, although some referred to me as a BuJew. Through the years, I occasionally lit Chanukah candles and went to a few Passover seders, and "break the fasts." Aside from that, I didn't give my Jewish identity much thought. Until October 7.

On that morning, I sat watching the news with my heart breaking in all directions. We had a friend visiting us from Atlanta (who was planning to go to Israel that November), and, like the rest of the world, we were in an utter state of shock. The events of that day had me reflecting on my own trip to Israel back in 2014 during a family pilgrimage. After visiting Yad Vashem, I was speechless and gutted. Something inside me was deeply moved as I felt my connection to my Jewish roots return and strengthen in a profound way. To say that trip was transformative is an understatement.

After the attacks of October 7, I decided I would light Shabbat candles for the hostages and others who couldn't do it for themselves. It had been ages since I'd lit candles—I even had to google the prayer. I started watching virtual Friday-night services on YouTube.

Several weeks later, on Friday, November 10, I lit my Shabbat candles, said the Hebrew prayer and another one, more personal and from my heart. I went back to the living room and resumed watching the news, which was on 24/7 in our house. About an hour later, I heard a strange noise coming from the kitchen. It sounded like something had broken.

I went to inspect the situation and was stunned to see that even though the Shabbat candles were still burning, both of my crystal candlesticks had cracked. They just shattered down their long stems. What made this particularly jarring, disturbing, and downright eerie is that November 10 was the eighty-fifth anniversary of Kristallnacht. I get chills every time I think about it.

The fact that these candlesticks, which I've used for years, shattered on such a significant night felt like a sign. I think God was sending me a message. Was God telling me that the world is broken? Maybe. Was God reminding me to never forget? Possibly. I have since replaced my crystal candlesticks, but I am back to searching, trying to interpret what God wanted me to know that night.

RENÉE ROSEN is a *USA Today* bestselling author. Her books have been translated into multiple languages. Her latest novel, *Let's Call Her Barbie*, will be published in January 2025.

Rebecca Raphael

Making the Potatoes of a Joyful Jewish Life

When I opened the glove compartment of this guy's car, under the crumpled 1991 Saab convertible manual, I discovered a yarmulke. As a Shabbat-loving single woman in my late twenties on a second date, I took that navy suede kippah to be a sign from *Hashem*. Clearly I had found my *bashert*.

For some, it's an electrifying caress or a romantic getaway that sends butterflies to all the right places. For me, a stack of dog-eared Jewish publications on a nightstand does the trick. A *kiddush* cup on the mantel that's been passed down from one generation to the next? Goose bumps. A family tradition of banging on the table in a rousing *Dayenu*? I swoon. My primal love language, the way to my heart and soul, is *Yiddishkeit*, a devotion to Jewish traditions and culture.

The skullcap-in-the-glovebox suitor figured that out. Early in our courtship, he left me a late-night voicemail belting out a high holy days melody he had sung as a bowtie-wearing sixth grader in his synagogue's junior choir. As we got more serious, he faux-casually mentioned in front of my ailing, religious grandma that his Hebrew name was Menachem Mendel, just like the Lubavitcher Rebbe. At our wedding, I reached the heights of ecstasy when, on bended knee, he surprised me with the traditional prayer of *Eshet Chayil*, declaring his commitment not just to me, his "woman of valor," but also to creating a home together bursting with Jewish joy.

As a child, time stood still when my father walked through our front door early on Friday nights, Shabbat flowers in hand, marking the beginning of our family's cherished time together. From building a sukkah out of threadbare sheets in our backyard every fall to gleefully dancing on Simchat Torah accompanied by Bracha, our shul's accordion player; from waving Israeli flags in Independence Day parades to a decade of summers at Jewish sleepaway camp, there were so many foundational memories I wanted to re-create.

I also spent my formative years watching my grandparents mourn the loss of their parents and siblings among the six million Jews who were murdered in the Holocaust. For many in my generation, the Shoah was a catalyst for Jewish identity, a responsibility to be vigilant about ensuring the survival of our heritage and our people. It was ingrained in me by the Jewish philosopher Emil Fackenheim, and by those of my great-aunts and uncles who miraculously survived Auschwitz, that in addition to the 613 *mitzvot* (commandments) in the Torah, there is a 614th to follow: We must not grant Hitler a posthumous victory.

Since becoming a parent, there is no mitzvah I have taken more to heart—certainly because I feel the weight of our history and am passionate about Jewish continuity, but above all, because I believe Judaism offers a road map for a purpose-driven life of goodness and joy. By keeping kosher, for example, before a morsel of food can even graze my lips, I am prompted to savor the reminder of who I am and where I come from. For me, Judaism is the lens through which we can cultivate gratitude, honor our ancestors, raise moral kids, navigate despair, mark time with meaning, see the dignity in all humanity, show up for one another, and try to leave this world better than we found it.

Just as my Jewish experiences anchored my sense of who I was in the world as I grew up, I try to infuse my own home with Jewish values, Jewish music, Jewish prayer, Jewish food, Jewish rituals, Jewish holidays, Jewish giving, and Jewish love. My therapist, an Orthodox Jew, has a saying: "If you want the house to smell like Shabbat, you've got to make the potatoes." It's a metaphor we use to talk about how the magic of living Jewishly doesn't just happen—not for me, my kids, or anyone. It takes work.

In the aftermath of October 7, I am doubling down on Judaism as a personal and communal toolbox for a life well lived. I blast Eyal Golan's "Am Yisrael Chai" throughout our home, organize Shabbat dinners for hundreds, attend rallies in support of freeing the hostages, and sound the alarm for Jews and non-Jews alike about the resurgent tsunami of Jew hatred. There are countless recipes for making the potatoes, I am learning, particularly when we are activated by trauma, motivated to articulate a newfound sense of Jewish pride, and longing for a sense of community amid our vulnerability. Volunteer trips to Israel are at capacity, friends have found their voices as political activists or social media warriors, parents are galvanized to confront both latent and blatant antisemitism in schools, and business executives are displaying moral courage and leadership.

As I bless our three kids on Shabbat, I think about the unbearable void at Rachel Goldberg-Polin's dinner table and pray for all of the hostages. We FaceTime our first cousins Goldie and Eldad, whose idyllic kibbutz life in the Gaza Envelope was shattered when Hamas gunmen tried to break into their safe room, where they hid with their three young children. And then we welcome Shabbat with joy. My husband sings *Eshet Chayil*, just as he did all those years ago. Our eight-year-old plays *Mah Tovu* on the piano, our daughter lights the candles with me, and our oldest son chants *kiddush* before heading out to basketball practice. That glove-compartment kippah from decades ago has since been replaced by one from our kids' b'nei mitzvah, bedazzled with rhinestones because our daughter wanted them to be sparkly. Our kids, it seems, have the ingredients to start making their own potatoes.

Just last week, my husband sent me a selfie of him spontaneously wrapping *tefillin* at Chabad. He still knows how to catch me off guard. For my upcoming fiftieth birthday, I'm holding out for a breathy, pillowside *Oseh Shalom*, and for a lifetime of making more potatoes.

REBECCA RAPHAEL is a writer and editor whose proudest professional moment is when Rabbi Elliot Cosgrove thanks her from the bima of Park Avenue Synagogue on Yom Kippur for editing his annual book of sermons. She is a book collaborator whose recent projects include *Family Values: Reset Trust, Boundaries, and Connection with Your Child* with Dr. Charles Sophy and *Fair Play: A Game-Changing Solution* *for When You Have Too Much to Do (and More Life to Live)* by Eve Rodsky. A former producer for Rachael Ray, Dr. Phil, and Katie Couric, Rebecca's work has also appeared in the *New York Post, Marie Claire, Seventeen, Los Angeles* magazine, the *Jewish Journal,* the *Jewish Week,* and other publications.

PART TEN

Represent!

Julia DeVillers

American Girl Dolls and Jewish Joy

M y twin sister, Jennifer, and I were thrilled when American Girl contacted us. Would we want to write three books for the new historical American Girl dolls? As middle-grade authors and longtime fans of this iconic brand (Jennifer had given my daughter her first American Girl doll when my son was born), this opportunity felt special. As twins, it was extra-special to help launch their first-ever historical twin dolls.

As Jews, we had no idea how extra-special it would turn out to be.

If you're familiar with American Girl, their historical line represents different eras, such as the Revolutionary War and the Depression. We were eager to know which historical era we'd be researching and writing. The reply: the 1990s.

The nineties is historical? Oy vey!

When the books came out, we weren't the only ones surprised by this. News headlines included:

- "New 'Historical Character' American Girl Dolls from the 90s Have Millennials Feeling Old, Dusty, and 'Disrespected'"
- "Reading Ancient Texts: The 1990s American Girl Doll Zine"

Unexpectedly, we found ourselves in the headlines for an additional reason. *Hey Alma* asked: "Are the New '90s American Girl Dolls Jewish?" The answer: yes.

The Jewish Telegraphic Agency put out on the worldwide wire: "Meet the Real-Life Sister Act Behind the Two New '90s Jewish American Girl Dolls."

We loved brainstorming the stories of Isabel and Nicki Hoffman with the American Girl team. We reminisced about Blockbuster, the Spice Girls, grunge, blow-up furniture, the dial-up modem sounds, and Pizza Hut's Book It— things kids today don't even know about. We landed on Y2K as the theme, covering the 1999 holiday season, and added Hanukkah to the plot.

As daughters of a dad who was a child Holocaust survivor and a mom who had been raised Quaker but converted to Judaism before we were born, we grew up celebrating both Christmas and Hanukkah with our extended families. This duality was a natural part of our childhood, as it is for many kids. We didn't anticipate the significant impact that interfaith doll characters would have, nor how timely their release would be.

The dolls and books were released in 2023, during the time of a dramatic rise in antisemitism. The dolls' representation, with their loving family including two parents of two cultural backgrounds, felt especially poignant.

American Girl has two Jewish dolls in its line, Rebecca and Lindsey. It offers wonderful Hanukkah merchandise (tiny gelt and a menorah, a "Love You a Latke" sweater, a dreidel for doll-sized hands). Our dolls center on Girl Power and the nineties era. Nicki Hoffman fears the Y2K "bug" and wears her plaid flannel and overalls, while Isabel Hoffman wears a Cher from *Clueless*–inspired outfit and is excited about the new millennium. They're celebrated as much for their nostalgia as for their unique personalities. And they celebrate Christmas and Hanukkah in their home.

One of my favorite sections of *Meet Isabel and Nicki* is in Chapter 2: Happy Hanukkah. It's the last night of Hanukkah, and the twins say the prayers and light the Menorah, and play dreidel and win gelt. Just like we did when we were growing up. My favorite line comes before the twins get their presents (journals and sparkly gel pens):

A shiver of excitement ran through her as she looked around her family, the candle lighting up their faces in the darkness.

Isabel and Nicki are fictional characters, but we hope they help readers of all faiths appreciate the specialness of celebrating Hanukkah with them. My friend Courtney reminded me that Jewish holiday toys are rare. Her son's playmates have Rudolph, Santa, Nutcracker dolls, and Elf on the Shelf. While there's Mensch on the Bench, there's no Queen Esther doll.

Now kids have two new dolls who celebrate the joy of Jewish holidays and being part of an interfaith family. Even children unfamiliar with Hanukkah or Judaism can experience Jewish joy through the books. When girls buy an Isabel or Nicki doll, they'll be sharing a piece of my sister's and my childhood that these days feels precious.

JULIA DEVILLERS is the bestselling author of books for kids and teens. She also sold a TV pilot to CBS inspired by her life, and her book became a Disney Channel movie, *Read It and Weep*. Her next book is *Meet Me at Wonderland*.

Corie Adjmi

Celebrating Jewish Diversity and Unity

S tatistics show that when Jewish people are known, antisemitism goes down. Stories are a way for Jews to be seen.

The setting of my novel *The Marriage Box* is the Syrian Jewish community in Brooklyn during the 1980s. While I didn't set out to write a book embracing Jewish diversity, it quickly became clear that readers wanted to learn about this unique and unfamiliar world. They were curious about Sephardic Jewish history, culture, tradition, and food.

During book talks, I often point out that representing a group of people, *any* group of people, as one thing repeatedly dehumanizes and doesn't allow the group to be fully known, paving the way for dangerous tropes and generalizations to emerge. The world has plenty of misconceptions about Jewish people already, believing stereotypes that we are greedy, aggressive, neurotic.

The orthodox community has an especially bad rap. Television shows like *Unorthodox* and *My Unorthodox Life* show women in oppressed communities who are sometimes abused, always trying to get out. And while it's essential that those stories are told, the orthodox community I describe in my novel doesn't look at all like what's portrayed in those shows.

With the Jewish population at just 0.2 percent, there are many people in the world who have never met a real-life Jew. It's critically important that we consider the stories we tell and the ways Jewish people are represented in books and film and on shows like *Curb Your Enthusiasm* and *Schitt's Creek*. We need those characters and their humor like we need our Holocaust stories, but we need other stories, too.

The more stories the better. Jewish people are not one thing. We are Ashkenazi and Sephardic. We have blond hair and black. We are orthodox, conservative, and reform. We are entrepreneurs and artists and doctors and lawyers and stay-at-home moms. We are from all over the globe. We are not all wealthy. And we are not all white.

Storytelling is a powerful tool. Stories not only educate and enlighten; they inspire and cultivate empathy. They build bridges connecting individuals and communities. Telling stories and showing the richness and vastness of our cultural and religious diversity is a way for us all to be seen and included.

We have lived through a remarkable time in Jewish history. These last few decades have been a period of security and peace for Jews in America, and it's now being called a golden age for Jews. Some of us were lulled into believing our status here in the United States was solid, that we'd be safe and belong, as an integral part of the American fabric, forever. Since October 7, we recognize that is not necessarily the case.

It's more important now than ever to make ourselves known. In our desire to be seen, honoring our differences is essential, but we must also highlight our similarities and the thread connecting us. Maybe it's our shared history or the blood coursing through our veins. Maybe it's the stories *we* were told, the values imparted, the songs and prayers recited—but we are united. Our unity is our strength.

The days of us staying insular, complacent, or judgmental are gone. We can no longer remain quiet or on the sidelines. Instead, we must ban together and be seen—wear our Jewish star necklaces and our *Bring Them Home* dog tags, too. Loud and proud, let's share our stories. Write as an act of rebellion. Insist on truth.

We need the strength of the entire Jewish community, because despite our differences, we are one.

CORIE ADJMI is the bestselling author of the award-winning novel *The Marriage Box* and the short story collection *Life and Other Shortcomings*. Corie's essays and short stories have won numerous prizes and have appeared in dozens of journals and magazines, including HuffPost, *Newsweek, North American Review*, Medium, Motherwell, and Kveller. The *Jewish Chronicle* included *The Marriage Box* on a list of best Jewish books.

David Christopher Kaufman

Judaism: 5,000 Years of #Diversity

I was recently asked a question so many Jews must also be asking themselves right now: How do we move on from here? How do we reconnect with the progressive groups and causes that Jews and Jewish institutions supported for so many years that have so disappointed us since the Hamas attack on October 7?

My answer was: You don't *have* to. Many groups have benefitted from the generosity of Jewish advocates and donors yet failed to reciprocate in our hour of need. Jews who are wondering how to rebuild bridges and reestablish alliances must accept that some are permanently severed. And that's okay; there are many alternatives within Judaism and the Jewish community itself.

Take Canadian real estate billionaire Sylvan Adams. Last December, when American college campuses were rife with antisemitism, Adams gave $100 million to Ben Gurion University in the Negev Desert town of Beersheba. It was one of the largest gifts of its kind ever—not just in Israel—and offered a viable alternative for U.S. billionaires outraged by Ivy League leaders who failed to take care of Jewish students.

This time has not been easy for me. I may be Jewish—very Jewish in many ways—but I've always been a bit of an unlikely Jew, and an even unlikelier Zionist. I'm also African American. I don't "look" the way most American Jews are expected to look, and I've spent my entire life—at least here in the U.S.—almost always as the darkest Jew in the room. I'm someone most other Jews rarely think of as Jewish. And this has hurt. Often intensely, but mostly as background noise—a cost of doing business, one might say, when the business is being me.

Due to my unique circumstances, I haven't always been into the whole "Jewish community" thing. I was raised part of a synagogue but don't belong to one now. I'm far more of a "Jew" than merely Jewish—part of a tribe that exists beyond the confines of space and time and memory.

But the horrors of October 7 have changed all this. Like so many Jews out there, I have never felt more Jewish. We must now lean into this heightened sense of Judaism when considering the bridge-building or reparative work that is ahead of us.

Before October 7, a collective sense of white guilt propelled many Jews and Jewish institutions into funding various other identity movements. But we must also turn our money and attention and passions inward. I certainly have. And I've discovered a whole new world filled with Jews—all kinds of Jews. At a time of rising assimilation and antisemitism, assuming that Jews look or act or pray a certain way is no longer a luxury our community can afford. Let's face it: We need all the Jews we can muster right now. And they are there to be found. Built into Judaism itself are the queers and Blacks and Latinos and Asians and feminists and social justice fanatics that we've supported outside our community all these years.

And guess what? *They're all Jews, too.* We don't need to look outside of Judaism for diversity or intersectionality—we have plenty of it here already. Just look at me.

Recent estimates put the number of Jews of color, like myself, at roughly 15 percent of the entire U.S. Jewish population. That's more than one million people.

We must expand the definition of what it means to be a part of our community. It means claiming the diversity that is everywhere within Judaism today.

American Jews who are committed to uplifting and elevating marginalized voices, go uplift and elevate *marginalized Jewish voices.* The folks who have been standing in the background, quieter than most, darker than most, poorer than most, but who are very much still Jews.

We can and should retain our commitment to inclusive principles—which are noble, just, *Jewish*—but apply them to Jews and Jewish environments. Seek connection with Jews who may not look or speak like you. Ensure that Jewish institutions no longer merely reflect an outdated, Eurocentric Ashkenazi view. Make concrete efforts at getting more "seats at the table"—but also make them Jewish seats. A Jewish table.

In my case, stepping into a larger Jewish world that has not always welcomed me and often refused to acknowledge me has been scary. But also liberating. Revolutionary. An embrace of an authentic me I never knew existed. And I've only just begun.

DAVID CHRISTOPHER KAUFMAN is a *New York Post* editor and columnist; a frequent contributor to *Air Mail*, the *Spectator*, the *Telegraph*, and the *Forward*; and an adjunct fellow at the Tel Aviv Institute.

Lynda Cohen Loigman

Writing Jewish Stories Today

When my debut novel, *The Two-Family House*, was published, every part of the process was new to me. I had never seen a publishing contract. I didn't know how hard copy editors worked. I was shocked by the length of time it took for a book to make its way onto store shelves. But perhaps the biggest surprise was that my story, like every other book listed for sale online, was labeled based on its genre and subject matter for the purposes of ranking and sales statistics. It sounds ridiculous to me now, but I truly did not know I wrote "historical fiction" until Amazon told me so. I'm sure I *should* have known that a story set in postwar Brooklyn qualified as such, but I hadn't given it any thought.

The Two-Family House earned other labels, too. It was not just "historical fiction," but also, more specifically, "Jewish historical fiction" and "Jewish literature." Of course, I knew that my characters—inspired by my own family—were Jewish. But I hoped that the story would find a broad audience of readers. The novel was about motherhood, marriage, and secrets. It was a multigenerational family saga that I hoped *every* reader would find compelling. Although I was proud to be a Jewish author, I worried that labeling my novel as "Jewish" might risk minimizing its appeal.

That worry, however, did not stop me from writing a second "Jewish" novel—a story of estranged sisters who leave New York to work at the Springfield Armory during World War II. The story of *The Wartime Sisters* focused both on the rift between the sisters and the camaraderie among the many women working at the Armory, who spanned a wide variety of religions and ethnicities. But because the sisters in it happened to be Jewish, it was categorized as "Jewish historical fiction" as well.

By that time, I had come to understand that while my novels were being read by people from diverse backgrounds, the support I received from the Jewish community was particularly robust and meaningful. My third novel, *The Matchmaker's Gift*, was perhaps my most Jewish of all—set in an immigrant Jewish community on the Lower East Side and peppered with all kinds of Yiddish expressions, Jewish history, and folklore. It is a book I am incredibly proud of, but it did not become the "breakout" novel I was hoping for.

As I wrote and revised what would be my fourth novel, *The Love Elixir of Augusta Stern*, I wondered whether I was doing something wrong. Was I limiting my audience and future success by writing only "Jewish" stories? Was I being pigeonholed? Should I consider writing something different?

And then October 7 happened, and all of my doubts fell away. In the wake of that tragic day, I was prouder than ever about my choices. Jewish stories feel more necessary now than ever before—not only to give Jewish readers books in which they feel seen, but to highlight our shared humanity.

Today, I feel a responsibility to continue writing Jewish stories—not Holocaust novels or wartime tales, but stories in which everyday people and families wrestle with universal challenges. As a proud writer of Jewish historical fiction, I hope that my words can somehow reach across the page to encourage compassion and understanding among readers of every background.

LYNDA COHEN LOIGMAN graduated from Harvard College and Columbia Law School. Her debut novel, *The Two-Family House*, was a *USA Today* bestseller and a nominee for the Goodreads 2016 Choice Awards in Historical Fiction. Her second novel, *The Wartime Sisters*, was selected as a *Woman's World* Book Club pick and a Best Book of 2019 by *Real Simple*. Her most recent book, *The Matchmaker's Gift*, was named a Best New Book by *People* and a Best Book of Fall by the *New York Post, Parade*, GoodMorningAmerica.com, and BuzzFeed. *The Love Elixir of Augusta Stern*, her fourth novel, will be published in October 2024.

Elyssa Friedland

Write What You ~~Know~~ Must

"Write what you know"—a stern warning lobbed at authors frequently—used to really irk me. I wanted to write about what interested me, not what the publishing industry said I was allowed to write. Flexing my creativity and expanding my knowledge were among the chief reasons I was initially drawn to fiction writing. Around me, I watched authors get canceled for "telling other people's stories" and for writing about things they hadn't personally experienced. I was scared to step out of bounds, feeling a creep of resentment every time I shied away from a theme or plot that might get me in trouble. This resentment vanished after October 7. I am now more than happy to write what I know. In fact, I am compelled.

So what do I "know"? I know what it means to be a Jewish woman in America. I know what it's like to spend a semester studying in Israel. To have parents who immigrated to the United States a few years after World War II. To have grandparents who lost everything when the Nazis came. I know about fasting on Yom Kippur and attending a Jewish day school. I know jokes from the shtetl and priceless Yiddish phrases. I know how to make a pretty decent challah. Over the course of five novels, I mined this material over and over, taking pleasure in channeling my identity but also feeling the constraints.

In early 2023, I began working on my sixth novel, *Jackpot Summer*, about a family who buys a winning Powerball ticket while gathered at their ramshackle beach house at the Jersey Shore. The family was Jewish, but with a generic last name (Potter). There were scant cultural or religious references. I leaned more heavily on the Jersey Shore setting (again staying in my lane, since I am a Jersey girl), but I didn't feel the need to highlight the family's Jewishness like I'd done so many times before. How many times could I write about gefilte fish?

All of this changed in the wake of October 7. For a few weeks, I wrote nothing, too stunned by the horrors unfolding to concentrate. I could hardly focus on my novel as the testimony and visual evidence of the rape of Jewish women was disbelieved and as vicious voices on social media blamed the Jews for their own mass murder. The disinformation alone was staggering.

When I was finally ready to return to work, the manuscript staring back at me no longer felt right. I made swift changes. The fictional Potters became the Jacobsons. I changed the opening scene to a gathering after a Jewish burial ceremony. I added mezuzahs, pastrami, a synagogue, and a bar mitzvah. I needed to remind my readers that Jews have humanity. We aren't violent perpetrators. And we aren't only victims. We are a people with a rich cultural history spanning thousands of years, beautiful traditions, and a values- and morals-based religious code.

After years wishing I could color outside the lines, I now find comfort and purpose writing about my religious and cultural identity. Not because the publishing industry says I should, but because it is imperative to show the world what seems like a basic fact: Jews are people, too.

ELYSSA FRIEDLAND is the *USA Today* bestselling author of six novels and a children's picture book. A graduate of Yale University and Columbia Law School, she resides in New York City with her husband and three children.

Beth Ricanati

*Braiding Ourselves Together: One Challah
at a Time*

My world—our world—turned upside down after the Hamas attack in Israel on October 7, 2023. This type of event, unfortunately, wasn't an entirely new thing for us Jews. Horrific, unspeakable tragedy has happened. Often. It is the fate of our history.

My reaction was to lean in to my favorite ritual: making challah every Friday. Since that day in October, I continue to experience the power of this ancient practice. In the mixing of the six ingredients, kneading the dough, and sharing the baked bread, I have learned how to take care of myself *and* take care of others.

The weekly ritual of making challah has been a part of my life for the past fifteen years and I have made thousands of challahs, all over the world. As a physician, this meaningful ritual has also taught me many lessons about self-care, being present, intention, and community. I was so motivated by what I learned that I even wrote a book about my experience: *Braided: A Journey of a Thousand Challahs*. Since then,

I have made challah with more than one hundred groups and organizations around the world.

After October 7, I have purposely chosen—even more than usual—to make challah across boundaries, with as many different people as possible, both Jewish and non-Jewish. While we stand side by side at tables substituting for a kitchen counter, our hands in bowls of dough, we come together and forge a common ground, regardless of our different backgrounds and experiences. We need that now, more than ever. I need that now, more than ever.

Exactly five months after October 7, I was an invited speaker at Rancho La Puerta in Mexico. On the first day of the workshop, our group had made the challah dough, gathered around a large U-shaped collection of tables, elbow to elbow, and where we could all see each other. We were a diverse group: a Jew from the Midwest, a yogi from India, and many others. We brought our different backgrounds and beliefs to the table and folded them together into the dough.

One day later, those twenty-five bowls of dough sat perched on a low stone wall, basking in the Mexican sun. I stood in front of them, hat on my head, water bottle in hand, and squinted into the bright sun. And smiled. Each bowl was different. In some bowls, the dough came nearly to the top, almost bursting out. In others, the dough had barely risen, despite containing the same ingredients. Never mind that they'd all spent the night together tucked in the walk-in cooler.

I continued to smile. I repeated my favorite lesson of the Challah Practice: "Perfect is the enemy of the good." The differences in the dough reminded me of the differences in the workshop participants themselves.

The irony of standing in the shadow of Mount Kuchumaa, a sacred and spiritual site of the Kumeyaay tribespeople in Tecate, Mexico, making challah dough—a Jewish bread that nourishes us not only physically but also spiritually—exactly five months after October 7 was not lost on me. The tribespeople believed Mount Kuchumaa to be the place from which creation sprang forth. An apt location for us to come together and create new understanding. In that moment, in the glare of the sun at the base of this sacred mountain, it felt like things just might be okay.

That evening, Friday night, after we had braided the dough together, then decorated and baked all of those beautiful loaves, we shared them with the larger Rancho La Puerta community. Looking around the large rustic dining hall, filled with people from different countries, states, ages, genders, and backgrounds asking for more challah, *por favor*, in the shadow of Mt. Kuchumaa, I smiled.

And I finally exhaled.

DR. BETH RICANATI is the author of *Braided: A Journey of a Thousand Challahs*, a finalist for the National Jewish Book Award, among other awards. She is also a board-certified internist who has worked at the New York-Presbyterian/Columbia Medical Center and the Cleveland Clinic, and now sees patients at the Venice Family Clinic in Los Angeles, one of the largest clinics in the country for the underserved.

PART ELEVEN

Quiet! The Rabbi is Talking

Diana Fersko

I'm Fine

I'm sitting with a friend in the common space of a Manhattan apartment building along with maybe twenty other New Yorkers. It's November, or maybe December, just a few weeks after the attack. In front of the room is a woman, probably in her early thirties. To describe her as a woman isn't the full picture. What she really is is a mom. Her kids aren't in the room, but you can just tell. By her calm voice, by her inner confidence, by her body. And she tells her story.

On October 7, she didn't know what was happening. She shows us the WhatsApp chats from her kibbutz. *Terrorists inside kibbutz,* one reads. Someone is calling for help. Someone else isn't responding at all. Her family hides in the safe room. It doesn't have a lock. She stands guard near the door with a kitchen knife and instructs her young children to watch episodes of *SpongeBob* over and over and over again on their iPad in order to keep them quiet. Her husband goes out and tries to save his friend. He can't. The family of four survives. Most of their neighbors and friends are murdered in their homes.

I'm a congregational rabbi and the author of a horribly timely book on antisemitism. But mostly what I am is a Jew. And I like to think I'm a good Jew. At the very least, I'm a trained Jew. I know how to do Jewish things. I know how to keep kosher, how to light Shabbat candles, how to pray, and how to visit the sick. And I know something else: I know how to listen to survivors.

So, yes, post–October 7, I travel around the country with my book and I talk. I talk about the history of antisemitism and how what's happening now is not new, but rather an update of something quite old. I talk about the fluidity of political parties and the Jews. I talk about the university system, about strategies to fight back. I talk about my unwavering commitment to Israel. I talk about the uncertain future of Jews in America and what might happen next.

But more than I talk, I listen. Because I know that listening is a moral, religious obligation for Jews.

"You know why God gave you two ears, but only one mouth?" a rabbi asks a group of children rhetorically, lovingly. "So we can listen twice as much as we speak."

Shema Yisrael, we say every day. It's a commandment to the Jewish people instructing us to *hear* the truth. For Jews, the act of listening is a holy thing. So hearing the stories of those who were there is religious, but it's also practical; it will help me fight the jarringly familiar onslaught of denialism about to come our way. And anyway, like many of us, I've been listening to stories of Jewish persecution and perseverance my entire life. So I tell myself I am going to listen, because I have to, because it matters, because it's the right thing to do.

I listen to a jewelry designer, taken captive by Hamas from the Nova music festival, tell me how she tried to make herself as ugly as possible so her captors would not rape her.

I listen to a farmer who lives near the Nova music festival tell me how he found women, naked, tied to trees. He cut them off of the trees, closed their eyes, said the *Shema*, and moved on, saving hundreds of Israelis that day. I listen to a volunteer from ZAKA describe finding women mutilated beyond recognition. I hear a police officer describe witnessing the aftermath of the slaughter of babies and the murder of grandparents.

And I do the same with the situation at home. I man an unofficial but constant antisemitism hotline. My friends, my family, and my congregants call, text, and WhatsApp to share their outrage and concern. A lot of the messages are about our educational system: *My child's school removed Israel from the map; I'm a teacher and my students are repeating antisemitic conspiracy theories; my child has a moment of silence for Palestinian children in elementary school each morning and nothing for Israelis; my daughter is coming home early from college, she just can't take it anymore.* I try to provide support, validation, and education as best I can.

I carry the stories with me. I hold them in my heart. I pray for the return of the hostages. I think about them when I rise up, when I lie down, and when I'm on my way. All the atrocities, all the outrage and confusion, all the fear, all the survival. I keep it with me, trying to understand.

My friends text me: "Mental health check in," they write. "How are you managing?" They are nice. I love them. Of course, I'm okay. This is a crisis and there is no time for my feelings, frankly. I have to listen and lecture and organize and strategize and I have to lead. And anyway, I'm a great coper and I do all the things. I exercise, I hug my children, I process. *Yes, yes, I'm fine.*

And then, in March, I walk off the plane and I'm in Israel. And for the first time in a very long time, I do something instead of listen. I breathe. I breathe and I cry and I smile. I feel relief and release. Finally, I have the freedom to not be fine. Because in Israel, the horror of that day doesn't need to live within me; it's out there for everyone to see. We can grieve, collectively, communally, publicly. I walk down the street in Tel Aviv. I see an art installation of bloodied teddy bears with black bands tied around their arms or heads. The vulnerability and the violence perfectly, horribly expressed. I don't need to carry the pain inside because Israel is carrying it for me, with me.

When I walk out of my apartment in Manhattan, I see pictures of hostages, but they are all torn down or defaced. In Tel Aviv, I walk to Dizengoff Fountain in the center of the city, and all around the fountain I see pictures of teenagers, just like our teenagers. A girl in a sundress, a boy wearing a gold necklace, a child's toy shofar. It's all out there, documented and displayed for anyone to see.

In Israel, I am free. I am free to acknowledge how horrific October 7 was. How broken I feel. How afraid, how fortified, and how enraged I am. And I start to do things. I pick strawberries from a field so they don't go to waste. I dance with strangers on Purim. I have drinks with my beloved friends in the middle of the night. I'm moving, I'm acting, I'm alive again. Staring out at the Mediterranean on the beach, overcome with gratitude, I hear the words of Hatikvah in my mind. Maybe I am starting to understand what it feels like to be a free people in our land.

DIANA FERSKO is the author of *We Need to Talk About Antisemitism* and the senior rabbi of the Village Temple in Manhattan.

Steve Leder

To Be a Jew Today

To be a Jew today is to remember that the Babylonians threw our babies off the cliffs of ancient Israel. The Romans used an iron rake to skin Rabbi Akiva alive. They wrapped Rabbi Haninah ben Teradion in a Torah scroll, placed wet wool over his vital organs to prolong the pain, and set the scroll on fire. Spaniards burned us at the stake.

"The Jews were taken wholly unaware and were slaughtered like sheep. Babes were literally torn to pieces by the frenzied and bloodthirsty mob" is how the *New York Times* reported the 1903 Kishinev pogrom. The Nazis turned more than 6 million of us into bone and ash.

On Erev Rosh Hashanah, three weeks before October 7, I warned my congregation that Nazis brought Jews to the ovens, but now our enemies can bring the ovens to the Jews. I have never been sorrier to be right. To be a Jew today is to live the newest chapter in the oldest of stories.

After thirty years of pulpit exchanges, MLK celebrations, teaching bible classes together, and friendly lunches, I asked the bishop of our "sister" church for a thirty-second video speaking out against Black Lives Matter Chicago and Los Angeles for their new logo of a paraglider swooping down upon NOVA, guns ablaze.

"Oh, I can't get into that man," he texted back. "The church is divided and I can't take sides."

To be a Jew today is to realize most people are better at virtue signaling than they are at behaving virtuously.

Today it's a challenge to speak out or you get canceled and lose followers. It's time to know the difference between murder and killing, between bravery and cowering in tunnels beneath innocents who deserve better. It's time to challenge the Jews of Hollywood to speak up, and to appreciate each person who stands with us.

"Yea though I walk through the Valley of the Shadow of Death, I will fear no evil," says the poet of the powerful and poignant 23rd Psalm, reminding us that we will somehow walk through this valley of shadows together—not remain in it forever. For what is a shadow, really, but proof of light? No matter how dark or long, a shadow cannot exist unless a powerful light still shines.

Hate is love obstructed, not love extinguished. Hate is not the end of hope, but the beginning of a battle against fatalism, summoning me to deeper faith, clarity, and courage. So I take an oath to a more beautiful tomorrow, even when—especially when—I am a Jew today.

STEVE LEDER is a *New York Times* bestselling author and a rabbi at Wilshire Boulevard Temple in Los Angeles.

Rebecca Keren Eisenstadt Jablonski

On the Honey

few days have passed since I returned from a meaningful mission trip to Israel. I was both volunteer-
ing in affected communities and bearing witness to
the atrocities of the October 7 Hamas massacre. Now, as I
reflect, I struggle with sentiments that remind me of the
wise 1980s song by Naomi Shemer, "*Al Kol Eleh* / On All
These Things." She sings about the duality of the Jewish life
experience. Like a prayer, she asks G-d to protect both the
good and the bad, like a blessing on both the honey and the
bee sting. The song's brilliance highlights that life in Israel
has always meant contending with joy and pain.

My experience as a young female rabbi in the New York
area can sometimes be as Shemer describes: sweet as honey
and stinging after sharp tragedy. I often feel pulled in two
directions. I'm from a traditional background, yet I strive to
keep our religion and its practice relevant. For many in the
Jewish world, I'm a living contradiction as a woman and a
rabbi; female rabbis are not universally accepted.

Since the Israel-Gaza conflict has escalated to full-blown war, I have seen increased interest in Judaism and Jewish practice, a *wonderful* development for the *worst* of reasons: the most heinous crime against the Jews since the Holocaust and the fever pitch of antisemitism in the diaspora.

Everything as an American Jew today feels like it has two sharp edges: pride and fear in our Jewish identity. I've seen families I serve hang new *mezuzot*, outward-facing doorpost casings containing holy parchment, thereby affirming Jewish practice and presence. I've also seen other families remove theirs in fear. I'm consumed by a deep desire to help Israel's population endure evacuation and trauma *and* the need to strengthen our own communities in the States that are grappling with vandalism, violence, and protests.

After feeling the vibrations of war in both Gaza and Tel Aviv, I'm caught in an empathy minefield. While I care deeply about the humanitarian crisis that affects ordinary Palestinians, I firmly believe their suffering originated with Hamas's terrorist actions.

My pride in the IDF is mixed with distrust, given the failures in intelligence and/or arrogance that led to the surprise attack of terrorists on October 7. My own decision to help on a volunteer mission with the Jewish National Fund contrasted with the pull to stay home and build my own Jewish family. After picking eggplants on farms and feeding soldiers on the trip, I realized just how much help Israel needs—my impact was just a drop in the bucket. I started out participating as an anonymous volunteer, but by the last day, I was answering Jewish legal questions and leading prayers as our group's nondenominational rabbi.

While I felt safe on my organized trip and expressed gratitude to the soldiers I met everywhere, my confidence shifted to alarm after the IDF missed a Houthi drone from Yemen that hit Tel Aviv six minutes from where I was sleeping, killing one man and injuring several others. For the next thirty hours that I spent in Israel, I marveled at the resilience of the Israeli population after such a brazen attack. Yet again, I wondered if Israel's casual ability to move on was because the people live in denial induced by a state of trauma. Maybe we all do as Jews.

When I feel lost, I often look to scripture for both wisdom and a glimmer of G-d. Luckily, part of my work is bar and bat mitzvah education and preparation, which keeps me close to the Torah. Harper, one of my longtime students, was a flower girl at my recent wedding. A spitfire twelve-year-old, she, too, is a contradiction: a loving girly-girl with pink fluffy blankets and yet a competitive lacrosse player. Her bat mitzvah falls in September 2024 and her corresponding Torah reading is Deuteronomy's Chapter 30, *Nitzavim*.

Harper and I had two Zoom lessons while I was in the Jewish ancestral homeland. It was awesome to work with the backdrop of the Holy Land while she joined virtually from a sleepaway camp in Upstate New York. During our second session, I wondered if I should tell her about the July 19 Houthi drone attack and the coincidental massive technical outage that wreaked havoc across the globe. Instead, we read her Torah portion: "I have set before you life and death, the blessing and the curse. You shall choose life, so that you and your offspring will live" (Deuteronomy 30:19).

In the same section of Torah, Moses laid out two paths. After recognizing the good and the bad always in their midst, Moses implores the Israelites to focus forward and actively seek the good. Moses admits that curses always loom and pessimism is an option. The challenge for us then and now is to take the right road. After surveying *kol eleh*, all these things, I actively choose the blessing mindset.

Admittedly, I occasionally feel sucked in by negativity and the muck of real danger. But, for American Jewry, for the Israeli population, and for me, the only way forward is to choose positivity. By doing so, I focus on the miracle of living my life as a Jew, a glass-half-full perspective on world Jewry, in spite of peril. I feel blessed to have recently prayed at the Western Wall; I feel heard by G-d and held by my people.

As a rabbi, I choose prideful expression, observance, and adherence to modern mitzvot. I choose to help Israel with money and action. I fortify myself against haters and threats. From this seat at the table, my cup actually overflows. Despite the conflict, I choose life and ask for the good-G-d's protection. Am Yisrael Chai.

REBECCA KEREN EISENSTADT JABLONSKI is a rabbi, author, and private educator. She obtained semicha from Mesifta Adas Wolkowisk in New York and graduated with honors from NYU's Tisch School of the Arts. She has spent more than fifteen years as an on-demand Jewish life concierge. Rebecca's debut memoir, *Confessions of a Female Rabbi: Relevant Religion in an On-Demand World*, was published in August 2024. She works with various synagogues and families all over the world and officiates weddings, bar and bat mitzvahs, funerals, baby namings, bespoke holiday gatherings, and other Jewish life cycle events. She serves on the board of Building Together: Building Relationships Between Palestinians and Israelis, and is involved in many other charities. She resides in New York City with her husband, Ben, and their Shih-Poo, Scout.

Sharon Brous

Invisible Threads of Connection

This trip was a long-planned fiftieth birthday winter break with the kids—now big enough to appreciate the beauty and some of the complexity of Vietnam and Cambodia. But after October 7, and my father's death just weeks before, my will to adventure halfway around the world had all but dissolved. I couldn't imagine leaving my mother in her raw grief, or my community, for that matter, in theirs. The thought of being far from home—which I generally would have found exhilarating—rattled me. I was filled with irrational fear. Several times I announced to the family: "We're canceling the trip. It's just not the right time."

But that's when I heard my father's voice most powerfully and clearly: *You are going.*

It wasn't just the idea of losing our deposit (though that alone would have flipped him in his grave). It was his determination that *life prevails upon us to live.* My father had died. We were alive. Israel was in anguish. Gaza was in ruins. We still needed to be human beings, to see beauty. To bike on dusty dirt roads with rusted gears while greeting every stranger with an upbeat *Xin chao!* To play increasingly competitive card games late into the night with our teenagers, as long as they'd have us.

Joy, I had to remind myself, was not a luxury, but a spiritual necessity.

So we went. The twenty-two-hour flight landed us in a wondrous foreign landscape, just as we had imagined. I worked hard to suppress the inescapable sadness I felt at having chosen destinations that didn't even have enough Jews to make a minyan, leaving me unable to say the Mourner's Kaddish for the duration of the trip. I was only weeks from launching my book, a testament, in a lonely and broken world, to the power of a loving community willing to hold you in your sorrow and say: *Amen! I see your pain. I will not run away from you!* And yet, there I was, struggling to honor my father's memory with love, ice cream, and Zoom minyanim at ungodly hours. Despite my public call to sacred presence, I struggled with the ache of absence.

That wasn't the only challenge on the trip. The beauty, adventure, and wonder couldn't mask that as the war in Gaza intensified, even some of the far reaches of the world were growing increasingly inhospitable to Jews. One of my daughters wore a gold *magen David* (Jewish star) necklace, a present from her bubbe for her seventeenth birthday, which she wore at home without hesitation. But in the bustle of the Vietnam markets, the necklace drew the attention of rounds of tourists who were either struck by the oddity of seeing actual Jews, or truly indignant to be sharing the Hanoi streets with us.

There were a few creepy moments, like when snickering tourists recorded videos of my kid as she walked down the street. Only once did we feel truly scared: when four men aggressively followed her and jeered her out of the shop where she was looking at linen skirts. We high-tailed it back to the hotel that night and sat our kids down for *the talk*, a real conversation about what it means to be a Jew in a sometimes hostile world.

"We're obviously proud to be who we are," we told the kids. "No ignoramus can scare us into taking off our kippot or Jewish stars. But . . . we have to be vigilant, especially when far from home. There's a time to slip the star beneath your shirt, or put on a baseball cap. We want to get home safely, after all."

I hated this conversation. I was deeply worried that I was getting it wrong. On one hand, I wondered: Would our careful vigilance essentially cede the public space to antisemites? Or, on the other: Would our stubborn Jewish pride get one of us hurt?

The next day, we got onto a boat to sail into the emerald waters of Ha Long Bay. A group of five people sat across from us and seemed to be staring at us with wild eyes. I saw one of them not at all subtly point to my kid's necklace, which was only partly obscured by her T-shirt collar.

The group started to whisper to each other: "Jews! Jews! Jews!"

That was it. We got everyone up and moved to the other side of the boat. (A boat! No escape!) My heart was pounding and my head spinning.

Moments later, out on the deck, a person from that group approached me. "Hey, I saw your daughter's necklace," she said. "Are you Jews?"

My body froze. "Yes," I said. *This is happening.* "Yes, we are Jews."

"Oh my God!" she exclaimed. *"We're Jews, too!* We were so excited when we saw your family that we literally started to cheer: 'Jews! Jews! Jews!'"

"You're *Jews*?" I repeated. "And you are five? That's fantastic! I'm saying kaddish for my father. Would you join us for a minyan?"

"We're saying kaddish, too!" she exclaimed. "For *our* father!"

Now we were both crying.

"We planned this trip," she said, "to mark the end of our year of mourning."

And that is how, in the midst of a world on fire, in the middle of a vast body of water known for its quiet grace with only limestone islands with rainforest peaks as our witnesses, ten Jews made a kaddish minyan in Vietnam.

I was so relieved my daughter hadn't taken off her necklace. This was precisely the power of presence I preached about, and the sense of community I so deeply yearned for. I had rediscovered the invisible threads that eternally connected me to my father, and to my people, too. Amen.

SHARON BROUS is the author of *The Amen Effect: Ancient Wisdom to Mend Our Broken Hearts and World*, a national bestseller, and the senior and founding rabbi of IKAR.

ABOUT THE EDITOR

Zibby Owens is the author of *Blank: A Novel, Bookends: A Memoir of Love, Loss, and Literature,* the children's book *Princess Charming,* and the editor of three anthologies: *On Being Jewish Now, Moms Don't Have Time to Have Kids,* and *Moms Don't Have Time To: A Quarantine Anthology.* Her next novel *Overheard* is forthcoming. A frequent contributor to Good Morning America and Kate Couric Media, she has contributed to *Vogue,* Oprah Daily, the *Washington Post,* and other outlets, and has appeared on CNN, CBS This Morning, and many others. *Vulture* called her "NYC's Most Powerful Book-fluencer."

Zibby is the CEO and Founder of Zibby Media, dubbed "the Zibby-verse" by the *L.A. Times,* which includes the award-winning, daily podcast *Moms Don't Have Time to Read Books;* the boutique publishing house Zibby Books; Zibby's Bookshop, an independent bookstore in Santa Monica, California; Zibby's Book Club; and Zibby Retreats, events for book lovers.

A graduate of Yale University and Harvard Business School, Zibby currently lives in New York with her four children ages 9 to 17, and her husband Kyle Owens, co-president and founder of Morning Moon Productions.

zibbyowens.com
zibbymedia.com
zibbyowens.substack.com
@zibbyowens
info@zibbymedia.com

ABOUT ARTISTS AGAINST ANTISEMITISM

Artists Against Antisemitism is a 501(c)(3) organization founded by a group of leaders who believe in spreading light to offset hate. The founding author team is made up of contemporary Jewish women writers from the U.S., but the extended community is for everyone: artists, creators, and supporters of all types, both Jewish and non-Jewish.

Their mission is to raise awareness of antisemitism, promote education about Jewish history and culture, and work to help build a kinder, brighter, more understanding future.

Anyone who wants to stop the rise in hate crimes, prevent more antisemitic attacks, and help the Jewish people through this wave of hatred is welcome.

theartistsagainstantisemitism.com
@theartistsagainstantisemitism

All profits will be donated to Artists Against Antisemitism.